SPOTTY THE BOWER-BIRD
AND OTHER STORIES

Spotty the Bower-Bird
AND OTHER NATURE STORIES

———

E.S. SORENSON

This edition published 2019
by Living Book Press
Copyright © Living Book Press, 2019

ISBN: 978-1-925729-97-9

All rights reserved. No part of this publication may be reproduced, stored in a retrieval system, or transmitted in any other form or means – electronic, mechanical, photocopying, recording or otherwise, without the prior permission of the copyright owner and the publisher or as provided by Australian law.

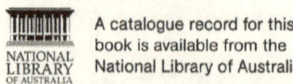

A catalogue record for this book is available from the National Library of Australia

CONTENTS

SPOTTY, THE BOWER-BIRD	1
QUIYAN, THE POSSUM	17
JACK, THE KOOKABURRA	33
WARRIGAL, THE DINGO	50
BLUEY, THE WREN	67
KOJURRIE, THE GOANNA	83
KARAWAY, THE COCKATOO	98
BOORABY, THE KOALA	116
BROLGA AND JABIRU.	130

THE BOWER OF SPOTTY, THE BOWER-BIRD.

(A. H. CHISOLM)

Spotty the Bower-bird.

PART I.

SPOTTY was a downy little chap with feathers only on his wings. He was squatting uncomfortably in a flimsy twig nest at the top of a gum sapling, when he took a first survey of his surroundings. The cavity of the nest was so shallow, that he had merely to raise his head to do this. His view in front embraced a mile-width of open forest, with a low sandy rise covered with Cypress pine beyond it. Close behind him were narrow strips of scrub that bordered the Warrego River. The winds came wilting from the stony plains of the Paroo. The landscape shone grey under the summer sun; but, to Spotty, whose eyes had but recently opened, it was all wonderful and beautiful.

There were other nests about, two of which he could see from his higher position. One, containing two baby birds, was in a needle bush at the edge of a thicket. The other, which also contained a pair, was in a pine tree further out. In a third nest, on the other side of the river, the eggs had only just been laid, though it was now December.

Couples had been busy nesting and rearing their tender broods since the beginning of October, not only in that particular neighborhood, but through out the interior parts of Victoria, New South Wales, Southern Queensland, and South Australia. The

Spotted Bower Birds favored always the arid mallee and brigalow country, and the tussocky inland plains that were interspersed with low bushes, small thickets, and scrubby ridges.

There was nothing important in his appearance, except that he looked a little odd with the prominent fleshy bare skin at the corners of his mouth, which, in his parents, was still thick and of a pinky color. For all that, he was unique in ornithology, since he and his dozen relatives, making up the group of Bower Builders, were the only birds that constructed, besides a nest, an ingenious playground or meeting hall. They were, in fact, the champion feathered architects of the world.

Some of the members of the group were more distinguished in certain respects than his own species. One, who lived in deep scrubs away over in Papua and neighboring islands, was the Gardener Bird, so called from the fact that his playground was a charming little garden of green moss, which measured nine feet across, and which was decorated with bright berries and flowers. Behind the garden, and opening on to it, was an elaborate little hut, or gunyah, composed mainly of orchid stems. It was eighteen inches high, built round a conical pile of green moss, and topped off with an orchid.

The Golden Bower Bird (who shared the Northern scrubs with the Toothbill and the Spotted Cat Bird) rivalled the Southern Regent in the golden splendour of his plumage, and, though the smallest of Spotty's relations, he built the largest bower of all, the sticks of which were piled up against two trees. One wall was eight feet high, bent over to form an arch, and the other about eighteen inches. It was adorned only with flowers, leaves, moss, and berries. Scattered immediately around were half-a-dozen gunyahs, each about nine inches high, built with the stems of grass or ferns bent together, and roofed with a horizontal thatch of twigs. The whole resembled a blacks' camp in miniature. Among and around these little cubby-houses, the birds ran when playing their curious games.

The Great Bower Bird (of the Northern Territory and Northwest) was the largest of all. He always decorated his bower with sea shells, no matter how far it was away from the coast. The Queensland Bower Bird (of the scrubby regions of the Gulf country) had the worst reputation, for he feasted himself whenever he could on chillies, paw paws, granadillas, guavas and mangoes, and sometimes he stole hen eggs, which he carried off in his claws. The Toothbill (of the North Queensland mountains), whom the blacks called Cherra-Chelbo, a mottled greyish-brown mimic with a serrated bill, who played alone on a leaf-carpeted clearing, which was furnished with a stone anvil for breaking snail-shells on, was the most retiring. His shy little mate laid her two dark-cream-colored eggs in a loose stick nest hidden away in a lofty tree.

Yelgan (the Regent Bird), who in his third year donned a beautiful coat of rich yellow and velvety black, was the most gorgeous and the most pugnacious. He often fought in the mating season until either he or his adversary was blinded or killed. He shared the Eastern scrubs with the Cat Bird and the handsome black Satin Bird. The latter assumed his splendid satiny blue-black coat only after several moults—about his eighth year. This was old age for Cowry, the Satin Bower Bird, for he lived only a year or two after donning his full livery. Before that, he was greyish-green like his lady-loves.

Despite all these wonderful relatives, Spotty could still lay claim to special notice. Among other things, his species was the boldest, and the most widely distributed.

His mother fed him on caterpillars, although her own diet at this season consisted largely of fruits and berries. Though other little bush birds might cry noisily for their meals, he was rarely heard to utter a sound.

He saw very little of his male parent, for that busy variety artist was much of his time at his bower, decorating it with any glittering trifle he could find, and holding solo concerts or maybe entertaining an odd visitor. Social gatherings were few and unexciting now, for most of the wives were busy with family cares. The big functions would come in the spring time, when the young bachelors would meet the little maidens with the more serious affairs of life in view, and there would be keen competition, much jealousy, and a few combats over the belle of the season.

But there was a lot of fun and gaiety in the bowers before that time arrived. As the young birds became fledged and left the nest, there were "children's parties," at which Spotty and those of his age made their first bow in society.

His youth was plainly shown by his lighter plumage, shorter tail, and his evident dependence on his mother for protection and guidance, as she led him one bright morning towards the assembly hall. The first thing he was aware of was a medley of strange sounds that alarmed him.

They all came from the place of meeting. First, the ring of a splitter's maul, then the chop of an axe, followed by the straining of wire and the hissing, buzzing noise of a captured cicada were heard; next the cries of the Noisy Miner, Babbler, Magpie and Crow sounded in quick succession. He thought many birds and other strange creatures were waiting to receive him. But, when he came to the bower, which consisted of two parallel walls of sticks and grass stuck in the ground, and which formed an arched avenue about nine inches wide, the floor of which was strewn with berries and pieces of glass and china, bits of rag and tin, silvery trinkets, and small sheep-bones, placed at each entrance like a door-mat, and the other objects classified in heaps—he saw only his male parent running through the hall, with his feathers puffed out. He soon realised that the strange medley of sounds were made by that superb mimic. With the exception of the Lyre Bird and his own cousins, Toothbill and the Golden Bower Bird, no feathered mimic could equal his father in mocking any bush sound that he heard frequently.

Spotty's dark brown eyes bulged with admiration and astonishment when he saw the beautiful ornaments. He pounced upon a brilliant bit of blue glass and ran through the gallery with it as the old birds did, then dropped it, and picked up something else. As the guests arrived, amongst whom were proud matrons accompanied by their sons and daughters, he became more gleefully excited. While the older males met and paid court to the females, he took upon himself the office of showing his young friends the wealth and beauty of the ancestral hall.

There was a period of exuberant mischief among them, which gradually evolved into some degree of order as the old birds, uttering often a scolding note, varied with an occasional stronger display of bad temper, mingled with them. These hysterical youngsters had to be taught the art of playing and dancing.

With a preponderance of youth and inexperience, the play was very much of a go-as-you-please affair. The birds darted among one another and through the gallery, performing all manner of capers and antics, picking up some ornament and running with it, or throwing it over the back while passing through. During these proceedings, one bird occupied an elevated post. He was on sentinel duty. The King of the bower, who was Spotty's parent, sometimes stood in the centre of the bower—to admire and to be admired. He bowed to the ladies as they danced before him.

At its termination, the sentinel dropped down from his perch, and the party broke up.

There were several other bowers in the immediate neighborhood, at one or other of which the parties reassembled from time to time. Some of these bowers were formed by making a passage through the centre of a big tussock of grass, and lengthening the walls, which were bent inwards. In the passage was the usual high platform of tightly-knitted sticks which gave strength to the walls.

The birds usually assembled about 10 o'clock in the morning, and played for an hour. "At Homes" were held daily and the greatest goodwill and friendship existed amongst the whole community.

Early in the morning and in the afternoon, Spotty was taken abroad in quest of food, and in search of new attractions for the playground. He would share the latter and remain with his parents until the following spring. He was partly fed by them for the first couple of weeks. He was heavy and awkward on the wing yet, and a short flight left him panting for breath. But, as his tail lengthened, he acquired more of the grace and speed of his parents, as well as their untiring zeal and almost unconquerable restlessness.

His main ambition these days was apparently to become a great mimic like them. Whenever he heard a new sound, he would listen with rapt attention and endeavour to repeat it, then practise it at every opportunity until he could produce a realistic imitation. One of the first sounds he had picked up was the bleat of a lamb. He had seen mobs of sheep almost every day since he first looked out of the nest in the gum sapling. One day, the boundary-rider heard the bleat as he was passing a clump of needlebush, and turned back to investigate. As he entered the bushes, Spotty greeted him with a resentful quiss-s-s, and flew away.

"Deuce take these birds!" said the boundary-rider. "That's three times they've had me to-day."

His favorite food was wild figs and mistletoe berries. He also frequented the quondong trees, but so much of the fruit was pulled green for decorative purposes that only a thin crop reached the deep rosy tint of maturity. Unlike his cousins, the Satin Birds, who travelled in flocks, his species, when it went to the fruit trees, or returning therefrom, flew one after the other. His companions were never many, except when they met at the bowers.

As he grew older, he roamed about a great deal by himself. He always returned ere dusk to the roosting tree of his parents.

He was the cheekiest of the Bower Builders, and so inquisitive that he would perch on a traveller's tent, and watch every act, while that person prepared his dinner. Afterwards, he would hop about on the ground picking up crumbs, and would even sample the liquid in the billy-can. If another bird came to share the morsels, he would raise his neck feathers and growl, or scold, like a little bully.

Two miles down the river was a selector's garden, where he found a few cultivated fruits that he relished. They included grapes, tomatoes and chillies. The latter he swallowed whole so that they would not burn his mouth. In the winter months, when he had to do more hunting than usual, this garden provided green peas, cauliflower, and other succulent morsels. In this way he varied his diet of insects and figs.

Here he learnt to crow, and to call up the hens like a rooster, as if he had some dainty to offer them. Then he would suddenly cry like an eagle, at which the deluded hens and chicks would rush for cover.

He was so intent on learning to mew that he got down dangerously close to the first cat he met, and only his inherent alertness and activity saved him from instant death. When, with thumping heart, he joined his parent, who scolded the cat from a safe distance, he had a claw-mark showing redly on his dusky-brown foot.

PART II.

The winter months had been comparatively dull. Now, with the warming spring days there was excitement in the community. Young and old appeared more sprightly, and became more restless and active. The playgrounds were cleaned up, and the accompanying bowers, damaged by rains and floods, repaired and decorated for the biggest social event of the year.

They assembled one September morning at the parental bower, and at once began a vigorous contest among the males for the favors of the opposite sex. Spotty had mingled with these from his very babyhood, but he had never noticed till now how very attractive they were. His neck-frill was raised with pride as one and another came to coquet with him.

He was a fine handsome fellow, between eleven inches and a foot in length, with a rich brown coat, mottled all over with dusky-red spots or bars, varied with spots of rich buff. The under surface was mottled grey, the primaries and tail were tipped with white. The latter was nearly five inches long. The strong thick bill, measuring an inch, was dusky-brown. The crown feathers were reddish-brown, tipped with silvery-grey. Across the nape was a beautiful band of longer bright lilac feathers, forming a fan-shaped neck crest of metallic lustre. He was not singular in the possession of this head-dress, for the Great Bower Bird, Eastern, and Guttated Bower Birds also had it, and all three much resembled him generally.

The females closely resembled him in feather colours, but they were almost entirely lacking the lilac neck plumes that gave him such a striking appearance as he strutted among them. In place of the friendship and sociability that had existed throughout the year, the bearing of the males towards each other was now stiff and hostile.

After a preliminary bowing and scraping the play or dance began. One picked up a piece from the collection and, with half-opened or trailing wings, tail spread, and head turned first to one side and then the other, like a lady trying to look at her train, danced into the pavilion, then tossed the piece backwards and ran out at the opposite end. Meanwhile the others were circling outside, some with ruffled feathers and dragging wings.

Spotty, the Bower Bird *(Teacher's College.)*

Spotty's Bower and Collection of Treasures.

When the plaything was tossed back, another picked it up and entered the hall to go through the same performance. This was presently varied by an old male throwing himself on his back and holding the object up in his claws. Another immediately snapped it from him and bolted, only to lose it in turn to a swift-footed pursuer. Some, between running and dancing, rolled on the ground, jumped up and down, sidestepped and performed other curious antics.

After a while all formed into a procession and ran through and around the bower, chasing each other with the utmost glee and enthusiasm. At the same time they mocked the cries of all other birds with whom they were familiar.

There was a trim little maiden there to whom Spotty had taken a fancy. Unfortunately, she was also admired by another young bachelor. The procession had no sooner ended than they came into collision. They flew savagely at each other. They struck with beak and claw, and tugged hard when either got a grip of his adversary. The others stood by, to watch the vigorous conflict. It did not last long, and Spotty came out victorious.

It was not his only battle, for disputes arose at other bowers. In the end he departed from the old run with the maid of his choice. He had already decided where they should live—a tussocky patch well screened by a bit of brush. He at once began preparations for the bower, for that important edifice had to be constructed before nesting began. It represented a prodigious amount of labor, which was shared by the willing and faithful bride.

First, a playground about six feet square was cleared. Then, in the centre of that, two parallel rows of clay and gravel were laid down, about six inches apart. Along each row tall shafts of silk grass, Mitchell grass and kangaroo grass in bloom were firmly planted, heads uppermost, and the tops bent till they overlapped. At the back of this lining, a dense wall of sticks, also stuck in the rubble, was built on each side, and immediately surrounded with a light ballast of well-trampled twigs.

This stupendous task accomplished, the inner walls were sparsely decorated with blue flowers and blue and yellow parrot-feathers. A few bones and pieces of blue and green glass, bits of emu shell, and green pine branchlets, formed the beginning of his museum. To bring it to the level of his parents' would require not the gleaning of a month, or a year, but of many years.

The bower was twenty-seven inches long, with an inside width of nine inches. The walls were each nine inches thick and eighteen inches high. When completed, the bone heaps or mats would add another nine inches to each end. These, composed mostly of the back bones of sheep, were put down in four even heaps, one at each side of the entrances and spread thinly over the outer passage. The total number at either end was ninety. Besides these, a mat of twenty-seven small bones, intermixed with quondong seed, was laid down in the centre of the avenue. As will be seen, a remarkable feature about it was the constant application of the number nine. There were variations in other bowers in the neighborhood, but (remembering that the collections were often in process of being added to) they were sufficiently near to show that the bird's favorite number was nine or a multiple of nine. In the choice of decorations he also showed a strong partiality for blue, white, silver, yellow, and green colors. Red he would have nothing to do with.

This bower was their future home, their place of resort at all times, but more particularly at that season when nature prompted them to reproduce their kind. There Spotty displayed himself before his admiring mate, and they had rare gambols together. If another bird appeared on the scene, he rushed at him with a savage gurr-r-r, and drove him off. His love was too strong yet to tolerate the presence of another male, while Mrs. Spotty was too jealous to allow another female to intrude. They were all in all to themselves these days.

At times he would chase her round the playground as if he meant to strip the feathers off her. He ended by picking up one of the materials in the bower, and uttering a soft note of invitation. When she did not respond, he raised his feathers and set off on another Marathon race round the bower. His eyes bulged with the excitement. This over, he stood with spread tail and expanded crest. He opened first one wing and then the other, and uttered now a soft quiss-s-s or a low gurr-r-r, and picked up as a hen does when calling her chicks, till at last the little mate went gently up to him. After a moment's billing and circling together he made a sudden rush, and they flew away into the trees.

The main interest now centred in the trees. Selecting a mistletoe bush, which hung in the branches of a myall tree, she built a frail, loose nest of twigs and sticks, thinly lined with grass and a few feathers. It measured nine inches by four-and-a-half inches over all, with an egg cavity of four-and-a-half inches by two-and-a-quarter inches. In the flimsiness and the simplicity of its construction, it was characteristic of nearly the whole group. It was a poor receptacle for the two wonderfully marked eggs that the little mother shortly produced. Long oval in shape, and measuring one-and-a-half inches by one inch, they were each marked with numerous hair-like lines of rich umber, like fine thread wound round and round the shell, crossing and recrossing, on a ground color of pale green. The inner surface of the shell was blotched with light grey, whilst both ends were comparatively free from markings. They were so singular in appearance, that a stranger would have thought they had been painted by hand. The eggs of the Regent, the Tewinya, or Fawn-breasted Bower Bird, and the Guttated species were similarly marked, but outside the group they were matchless in their curious tracery.

Incubation occupied a little more than a fortnight, and the

twins were about three weeks old when they left the nest. When they could fly tolerably well, they were taken to the bower, which henceforth was the common daily resort.

Spotty had now lost his jealousy. Instead of shooing a casual caller off the premises, he made himself quite agreeable to him. So the old desire for company returned, with the resulting rounds of socials and pantomimes.

Every time he came to play he brought some decoration for his bower, and in the course of time it became quite a little curiosity shop. Flowers, leaves and green berries (placed in heaps like eggs in a nest) were removed as soon as they withered and replaced with fresh ones. He was often to be seen there at daybreak, arranging and rearranging his collection. A great source of annoyance to him was Sandy, the black-fellow, who made it his business to search the bowers for pipes, coins, pocket-knives, gold, opal, diamonds, brooches, pins, rings, and other valuables stolen from camps and houses, or picked up in the bush. In the process of searching, he scattered the bones, glassware and old china, as well as the hakea seed and quondong stones, all over the place—a liberty which Spotty hotly resented. When the disturber had gone, he ran about with ruffled feathers, scolding and growling, then busily set to work and put everything in place again. His numbers, however, were apt to get out of order on account of such interference.

White men occasionally chanced near his bower, and an odd one, out of kindness, would add something to the collection. But all such additions Spotty threw out with scorn, even though they were such as he would gladly pick up if he saw them lying about a camp. He did not vanish, like some of his cousins, at the sight of man, but from a safe branch would frequently utter his saucy scolding note when his haunts were intruded upon.

During a long period of peace, he acquired many choice articles that made his friends' eyes shine with admiration. But, though they might be envious, no respectable Bower Bird would steal from another. Among the assortment was a silver spoon which he had taken from a bench at the back of the selector's house; a thimble, stolen from a stretcher on the verandah of the same place, where the woman had temporarily put down her sewing, and a small pocket mirror that had belonged to a shepherd. This was his proudest possession, and was allotted a place to itself. A thousand times he had circled round it, trying to solve the mystery of the bird inside that did everything he did. Now and again he endeavored to look under it, and even turned it over. It was a great mystery, a most fascinating thing, and a wonderful treasure.

Still he accumulated things. In a jaunt along the scrub, his roving eye detected a glistening object lying on the bunk in a traveller's tent. The traveller was down at the river washing his clothes. By the time he had finished, Spotty was with his family at the bower, gloating over the possession of a silver watch and chain. When, after the morning's play, he returned to the tent, the traveller was still feeling his pockets, and looking through his things. Still searching up and down, he repeated for the hundredth time: "I'm positive I left it on the bunk." At last he settled down in the tent for a smoke. Almost immediately he heard the chock-clock of dray wheels overhead. This brought him out instantly. He looked all round, and even in the air, but all he saw was a brown bird perched in the tree overhanging the tent. He was unused to the bush, for he had only recently left the city in the hope of picking up a job at the shearing sheds.

He returned to the tent with a puzzled look.

Hardly had he sat down, when he heard the plaintive mee-ow of a cat on his roof. Out he darted again. Still there was nothing but the brown bird in the tree.

He went back, looking worried.

A minute or so later a lamb bleated two or three times overhead, followed by the barking of a dog. Surely this was no hallucination. Out again; a more careful survey of the surroundings; and still nothing but the brown bird in the tree.

He retired, nervous and desperate-looking.

Spotty, being of a prying, inquisitive nature, was interested in the doings of this person. He had also learnt by long experience that such places were worth watching. It was also too hot to be roaming about. So he remained perched in the shade, and to pass the time he presently gave a realistic imitation of a cock-crow. Chummy started and turned pale.

He held his seat and breathlessly listened. The crow was not repeated, but in a little while he heard a baby crying, followed by what appeared to be a woman saying "sh, sh, shh!" He was outside in two leaps, but his wild, wandering look found nothing but the brown bird in the tree.

That finished him. "This place is haunted," he said.

And out he got at once.

For ten years Spotty led a busy, active life, and no doubt he made a lot of fun out of it. Then, one day, a smothering duststorm caught him in the open in his old age, and, though he tried bravely to fight his way home, it was too late, and the hot, suffocating, darkening dust clouds swallowed him up. When old Sandy next went along the Warrego, seeking valuables in the treasure houses of the little thieves, the bower was deserted.

QUIYAN THE POSSUM

PART I

QUIYAN, the grey Possum, came to realise the stern realities of life in the dawn of a Spring morning. He was a pretty little ball of fur as he lay snugly coiled in his mother's pouch, his pink nose buried in the folds of his own sleek body. It was getting light, and he wanted to sleep. Time after time he snuggled down, but only to move restlessly again, and wonder why his mother was so still and cold. Then he put his head out, and saw that she was hanging by the neck from a pole which was leaning against the tree where she had been feeding. Looking around, he noticed similar poles set everywhere through the great forest, and, under many of them, Possums were hanging, with a noose round their necks.

While his pretty, round eyes were still staring in affright, the trapper came quickly through the bushes behind him. He had never seen a man before, but instinct told him that this monster that walked on its hind legs was an enemy, and he made an effort to wake his mother, to hurry her home. The trapper, grown callous in his work of slaughter, dragged him out by the neck. He would have thrown him to the waiting dogs, but Abe, the trapper's son, came up and said he wanted him for his cousin Joe, who had written to ask for one.

Abe handled him tenderly, and, after admiring his dainty hands, and stroking his soft fur, tucked him under his arm. In this position, Quiyan was taken the round of the traps. Later he came to know much about the dreaded trapper and his work.

The artful trapper took advantage of the possum's preference to come headfirst to the ground by the easiest incline. So he rested a pole against the trees on which he found claw-marks, and fitted it with a wire noose suspended to a stronger wire to keep it in position. Into this noose the possum put his head as he walked down the inclined pole.

The trapper started out early so as to beat the crows and hawks. He skinned the dead possums and reset the traps as he went. The rest of the day was spent in pegging out the skins at the camp, packing those that were cured, and making fresh pegs and snares. When he shifted camp, these snares made a cartload in themselves. His wife and children, living in tents, shared with him the lonely forest life. Besides horses and a serviceable vehicle, they had a couple of cows, which were milked in a rough bail rigged in a sapling yard. A flock of fowls was also kept, but the much-travelled hens had frequently to make new nests in the middle of their laying. A low tree near camp suited them to roost in, but Buckandees (native cats) and bushy-tailed rats gave a lot of trouble. The worst foe of the trapper, however, was the Dingo, who stole his possums at night. The struggling of the animals when caught often caused the pole to fall, and even when it retained its position against the tree it was not always safe.

Scores of young possums like Quiyan were torn ruthlessly from the parent pouches, but none of them were brought to camp to keep him company in the box Abe had made for him. The naked "joeys" made dainty morsels for the trapper's dogs, while the furred ones were liberated so that their skins, by-and-bye, might return him half-a-crown to half-a-sovereign each.

The trapper found them in all stages of growth, from a lifeless-looking atom, no bigger than a peanut, which had been placed on the teat by the mother, shortly after it had been born. This was usually about June. For a long time that speck of life was fed automatically, and was held on by a little bulb on the end of the nipple. This formed after the hard and pointed nipple was placed in the mouth. Thus, once removed in its embryo state it could not be replaced, and so must perish. The pouch, which was at first small, and the opening narrow, now developed quickly. The "joey" was as big, or bigger, than a new-born kitten before the fur began to appear. About the same time it became a separate, self-feeding animal. It then showed considerable activity and its growth was rapid. Soon it found the snug quarters, where it had snuggled for months, getting cramped, and had some difficulty in turning round, while the mother's movements were hampered with the increasing burden. She did not travel much these days, or climb any more than she could help. Still she did not yet cast the little one forth to look after itself. For a time it looked out of the pouch at the great strange world around it, while its mother fed it or sat purring on a limb, and its first taste of gum leaves was obtained while still in that snug retreat. At first it came half out, then it left the pouch for short periods.

The days in the nursery were now soon over, for the young one became too large to carry. Still, he was not turned away from the parent roof tree with a mother's blessing and not a gum leaf in his pocket, for he would probably go about with her, and share the nest with her, until the next season. At that time, his father, who had been away, reaping a planter's crop and neglecting his home and family responsibilities, would return and kick him downstairs. In these times, when it was a strenuous matter to exist, with so many foes around, and the full splendour of the ancestral forests a mere dream, the father, who had no burden to shackle his wandering feet, very often did not see his child. Not that he wanted to see him very much, or would recognise him if he met him at dinner, but the mother was widowed—or she married again. In either case, the little one had to go for good, and find a hollow for himself. With the continual thinning of forests, this was not an easy matter, unless he went away into new country. Many eventually did so.

In due time, Quiyan was delivered into the hands of Joe Grimby, who lived on a farm on the Richmond River. Though possums were numerous in the neighborhood, Joe made a great fuss over the orphan. His sisters, who were older than Joe, made more fuss still. They said he was a dear little creature, and they laughed till the tears came into their eyes when he hugged Joe round the neck, or clung to his matted hair. Their shrieks and contortions of delight astonished him at first, but they treated him so gently and caressingly that his timidity soon wore off. Indeed, he became ere long a cheeky and mischievous little imp.

Joe built him a large cage, with a dark corner in it, where he could snuggle up in soft corn husks, and fed him on gum and wild apple leaves, fruits and grain, varied with damper, cooked corned meat, and sugar. He was provided nightly with a clean saucer, from which he lapped milk and water with gusto, and sometimes sweet black tea.

Joe brought him to table with him at tea time, and, when a piece of bread was offered to him, he put out his pretty little paw for it, and sat up to eat it like a human being.

He took kindly to Joe. He would perch on his shoulder and purr, and, when he found the opening in Joe's shirt front, he liked him better than ever. Joe was his new mother, and here was the pouch he had so long missed. He got half into it, but his sharp claws touched Joe's ribs, and he was violently ejected, while Joe danced, and his sisters went into hysterics. This astonished him, and he desisted. Still, he was satisfied with Joe. He was evidently a marsupial of some kind.

Joe's father, however, he regarded with suspicion, for he was a fierce-looking monster like the trapper. Grimby treated him with good-humoured indifference, until an incident one night raised his ire against Quiyan and all his kind.

Grimby was having tea, and discoursing un-learnedly, to his admiring family, on the nationalisation of coal mines, when Quiyan, who latterly had been allowed the freedom of the house at night time, sprang down from the wall-plate on to the old man's bald head. The roof-lifting roar that came from Grimby, and the jump he gave, caused his good wife to drop the teapot on the cups, and the baby to topple off its high stool. Quiyan was so startled by all this, that he leaped on to the table, where he sat with his tail in the butter, and stared at the monster. Joe snatched him up, and disappeared for half-an-hour. When he returned, his father was able to deliver himself more calmly on the situation.

"You get rid of that little beast, Joe, as soon as you like, or there'll be a row. The idea of making pets of possums on a farm! One of the greatest night pests we have—next to wallabies, and parrimallas, and bandicoots. Look down the farm now! Round every tree and stump the corn's stripped."

Joe could not but admit that in such localities the possum was content to take up his residence in a dead tree, or even in the root of a stump, to save travelling. His rambles at any time never took him far from home. He must have trees, and, when they went, he had to go too. Joe humbly suggested that the best remedy was to move the trees.

"What," asked Mr. Grimby, ignoring the suggestion as beneath notice, "what does he do in the wheatfields? He hadn't been very long acquainted with wheat, but he soon showed ability to adapt himself to circumstances. He couldn't climb the wheatstalk, so he nibbled at the bottom till it fell, and ate the head of grain on the ground. In the barn he did better, and, making his abode on a wall-plate now and again, showed a desire to live there.

When he found a stack of bagged wheat, he made his presence felt more than ever. He called his kind to the feast, and they feasted. They spent the night there, for the heaped bags were just fine for racing over between meals, and for mischief, and doing handsprings, and playing leapfrog. In the morning the farmer found holes eaten in his bags, and wheat scattered all over the place. And you want to set him up in the house, and make a pet of him!"

Like most Australians, Joe had a warm spot in his heart for the nimble possum, and he had no sympathy with the hunter when the hunted scored against him. The grey possum, he argued, was a frisky, sportive little animal when not seriously molested, and he was inquisitive, fond of sweets, and always on the lookout for a change of diet. These propensities often led him into mischief, but he was not a pest any more than the horse, or cow, or pig, or the fowl, any one of which would do more damage if it got at a wheat stack.

Quiyan was kept in his cage that night for his own good. Mr. Grimby was a fussy, nerve-sensitive man at best, and a gambol so soon after the tea-table episode would be fraught with peril. But the following night, when everybody had gone to bed, Joe let him out. He first closed all openings about the house, including the chimney top, so that the possum could not get away into the bush. He put some green leaves, bread, sugar, and water near the cage to keep him from rambling; but he rambled all the same.

Joe was awakened by the falling of the clock, and immediately afterwards two glass vases clattered down and smashed. Joe knew at once it was his pet, and, hearing a commotion in Grimby's room, together with some remarks befitting the occasion, he slipped out quickly to capture him before his father found the matches.

A great clatter of falling tins and a bottle of spirits from the mantelpiece guided him. He captured the little mischief, and regained his room as Grimby fell over the rocking chair. Then, while the latter fumbled and groped about, he opened the back door, hauled the cat in, and returned to bed.

By the time Grimby had found the matches, the cat was purring round his legs It got a reception that surprised it, while Mrs. Grimby was soundly rated for shutting up the house without putting the cat out. Nothing was said about the possum.

Next night, Quiyan was kept in again by way of punishment. But he managed to get out, and the window being up, he was very shortly viewing the situation from the top of a post. The bush was calling, calling. Again, he was dissatisfied with a mother who slept all night, and only got up when it was time to go to bed. He jumped down, and bounded away into the world of trees.

PART II.

A squeak in the distance told him of the presence of other possums. He stopped once, with a sharp stab of fear, as a squirrel darted over him with a sudden squeal, and his heart fluttered painfully when a dingo howled quite close to him.

Just as he reached his fellows, many of whom were gambolling on the ground, they made a wild scamper for the trees. Pausing a moment, he noticed that none of them rushed straight up on reaching a tree, but darted partly round it first. Instinct told him that danger was hot-foot in pursuit, and in terror he fled likewise. They were high up among the branches in a few seconds, but Quiyan was very young yet, and his gymnastic exercises had been neglected. Desperately and laboriously he climbed a few feet, then he almost dropped off with shock as a brute like a dingo leaped at him from the grass. Trembling with fright, he struggled to a limb and crouched down beside an old buck, who was purring defiantly at the enemy.

"What is that?" he asked.

"A fox," said the veteran.

"When I was young like you there were none of them about, but now they are plentiful, and they are worse than the wild dog. They lie in ambush, and when you go down they spring out and catch you. You'll have to keep your eyes open, young one. Where is your mother?"

"She was caught in a snare a long way from here."

"The old sad tale!" said the veteran. "Where do you sleep now?"

"I haven't found a place yet," said Quiyan. "I must look for one to-night."

"Better be smart, young one," said the veteran.

"If the man foe sees you in the day, he will shoot you with his gun. The most terrible of all our enemies is the man foe."

Quiyan shuddered, and his pretty eyes filled with tears.

The fox went away at last, and then Quiyan descended and began his search for a suitable hollow. Dozens of trees he climbed, pausing now and again to refresh himself on various leaves, and on choice bits of herbage and sweet roots between trees, but what hollow knobs and spouts he found were already occupied. The occupiers were seldom at home, but they were never far away.

QUIYAN, THE POSSUM

(B.J. Lane.)

THE GREY POSSUM. *(A. H. Mattingley.)*

He entered one, which appeared from the cobwebs in the corners and the dust on the floor, to be deserted. He was, however, almost immediately ejected, and knocked head over heels off the balcony. This made him wary, and, though considerably shaken and discouraged, he continued his search.

The dawn still found him searching. He was then on a treeless flat. He stepped gingerly and miserably through the wet grass, and in terror of his life. What chance would he have if the fox appeared now? There were other foes which he had not yet encountered, but which he came to know later. There was the carpet snake, which every possum dreaded, for he could not always hear it in the grass, and it often threw its deadly coils around him before he was aware of its presence. Though the dingo could find him anywhere by following his scent, he gave warning of his approach, and the possum could escape. However, he was not always so fortunate, he was a poor traveller on the ground, though he could spring around and side step with marvellous agility. If no friendly tree was handy, he fell an easy prey to the dingo and the tiger cat. In the air were the Eagle and the great Brown Hawk, which might swoop suddenly upon him and carry him off in their powerful talons.

He made all haste to the first clump of trees, which was on the bank of the river, and, choosing a bushy sugar gum, clambered wearily up on to a limb. When the sun peeped through his arbor, he was trying to sleep under difficulties, and soon his eyes were tear-wet and sore with the fierce light The Noisy Miner and the Tallarook (Wattle Bird) discovered him, and these made such a noise that other tormentors were attracted. They seemed to recognise his plight, and therefore persecuted him for hours. The worst were the Kingfisher and the Magpie. He grew tired with dodging and ducking as they darted at him, and sometimes he put up his hands to ward off an attack. The vicious snap of the Magpie's beaks, which missed his ear by only a hair's breadth, so alarmed him, that two or three times he almost fell off his lodging.

"This will never do," he thought, looking dejectedly around; "I must get a house to-night if I have to fight for it."

He went higher up the trunk, where he sought the shelter of clustering leaves. Above the first branches there were several knobs like huge warts, and in one of these, to his great joy, he found a cosy hollow. There was no danger of being knocked up here in the middle of the day, for all possums had long before this returned from their meetings and banquets. This hollow had no owner. It was his, and in it he curled up and slept.

For a few months he occupied that comfortable hollow, content to live alone, though he mingled awhile with other possums at night. But there came a change as he grew to maturity, a strange restlessness that drove him to seek companionship, and not the companionship of his own sex. With these he fought fierce battles, till his ears were scarred with tooth and claw. In most cases the cause of the battle was a coveted doe. The time was April, the month when possums mate. On a leaning ironbark, he had met one who welcomed his advances, but his love-making was soon interrupted by a rival. There was a short, sharp tussle on the bent trunk, which ended in a sousing fall for both. Limp and sore, they sat awhile on the couch grass, where they sparred and snarled. Then the rival decamped, and Quiyan returned quickly to his waiting partner.

For a long time after that he was absent from his home, for he slept with his mate by day in another hollow. When he returned he found that Kooragai, the Ringtail Possum, had jumped his claim, and he had to look again for another domicile.

Besides Kooragai, he had several other relatives, most of whom he never saw. Among them, the Black Possum, who belonged to Tasmania; the Striped Phalanger, of Northern Australia, an exceedingly pretty little creature, having parallel black, or dark brown, and white bars running the length of his body; the Mulbenger, of Western Australia, who had a long snout and a serrated tongue, with which he extracted the nectar from the honey-cups of the eucalypti; the Tula, a Queensland ringtail, who, like the Koala, the native bear, was often abroad in daytime; and Koorooi, the Sombre Ringtailed Possum.

Quiyan very rarely fed in the same tree in which he slept. On emerging at dusk, he noted carefully what was going on below, then tidied himself for "going out." He washed his face and combed his fur, licking his paws, and using them in the same way as the domestic cat.

His first act on going downstairs was generally to drink. He then spent some time on the ground, fossicking about for yams and fruits before joining his fellows for a frolic. Often a score or more gathered in one tree, and remained there for hours. With the approach of dawn they scattered for their holes.

In the hot summer months, Quiyan lost his sleekness and good looks. He was poorer and his fur was thin and falling out. He slept more now. Only a yearning for a ripe banana, or a feast of green lucerne, could take him far from home. Once he came across a tent, which had been pitched by some timber-getters under a low ridge. Here he discovered flour, sugar, raisins, and a tucker box in which was much that suited his palate. He chewed holes in all the bags, and sampled their contents. When he repeated the visit, the timber-getter was waiting for him, and he chased him hotly from tree to tree. The man uttered terrific yells, and lashed at him with a long bullock whip. Three different trees he made desperate attempts to ascend, only to be whipped off when he had got several yards up. When he at last escaped the terrible whip, and, perched panting in a silky oak, the timber-getter hurled blazing fire sticks at him. Twice he was knocked swinging off his perch, but was saved each time by his long clinging tail. He was so terrified and had so many sores and aches, that he never went near that tent again.

When the cold months returned, he had put on a new coat, which was firm and thick. With his gay appearance came gaiety of spirits.

This season he had a new mate, for his first had been captured by a black man. Her furry coat, which he had so often admired, was now carried by the wandering lubra.

He had most reason to dread the blacks by day, for it mattered not how high the possum was, or how well selected the hollow that formed his nest, they knew by the number and age of the claw marks on the soft bark that he lived there. They climbed up with tomahawk and vine and cut a hole in the wall of his bedroom, through which he was roughly hauled out by the tail, then battered against the tree trunk, and dropped to the ground—dead. The flesh was their favorite meat, and the furry skin their best material for making rugs to cover them in cold weather.

Ever as the seasons came and went, the settlements grew thicker and the forest thinner, till at last his own tree was sent crashing through the brush on the river bank. When he scrambled out of the debris, dazed and bruised, he had a wild race for life from the axeman's dogs. Being hot pressed on the brink, he sprang into the river and swam hard for the opposite bank. He swam fairly well, though he had never been in water before. The dogs beat about and barked for a moment or two before they followed him, and thus he landed with just time enough to spare to get up a convenient lillipilli. They squatted under the tree, where they barked at him for half-an-hour. However, as the men had no boat, he was let off.

That night he trekked still further afield, and found a new home in a strange forest. Here there were hundreds of his family, who frolicked on the boxwood flats between a high ridge and a broad lagoon. He was a happy, contented possum thereafter, playing and feasting the night long, though he had many adventures and some narrow escapes. At first two other possums had their abode in the same tree as himself, though in a different spout. The man with a gun, who walked abroad on moonlight nights, shot them both. He remembered every detail of the shooting: the man mooning round the tree until he had got the foolish possum in the full face of the moon, the flash and roar of the gun, the thud of the victim, as it reached the ground, and its agonised cries as the dogs pounced upon and worried it.

Descending warily that same night, he found a mother Koala sitting at the butt of the tree, with a baby on her back.

"I wonder you didn't fall," said the Koala. "Do you always come down headfirst?"

"Of course," said Quiyan. "Don't you?"

"No; I descend backwards. It's easier."

"Do you go up backwards?" asked Quiyan.

The mother Koala gave a loud snort, which woke the baby and made Quiyan jump.

"What an idea!" she exclaimed, chuckling in a koalaish way. A stertorous cry down the flat interrupted her.

"That must be the old man," she said, listening. "I haven't seen him since the afternoon."

"Do you go about in the day?" asked Quiyan. "He does. He's out at all hours. I must go and see what he's doing." Saying which, she dropped on all fours and went off slowly down the flat. Quiyan darted away in another direction, where he knew there were some young lady possums, who would console him for the loss of his friends.

One day a piercing shriek, which startled the birds on land and water, rang through the forest.

Quiyan, rudely awakened by a scratching at his door, had looked up to see Kojurrie, the goanna, stealing into his bedroom. Lacking the shrewdness and cunning of the platypus, he had only one opening to his domicile, and thus, when the black robber thrust his head in, his exit was cut off.

With his back to the wall, he hissed and sparred at the approaching foe. His eyes were aglare with horror. The goanna rushed through his guard, and, seizing him behind the shoulder, dragged him out, despite his shrieks and struggles. A frantic plunge lifted Kojurrie off the limb, and both fell heavily. The struggle was continued on the ground, while Magpie Larks and Gillbirds, attracted by the commotion among the dead leaves and twigs, chattered excitedly on adjacent limbs.

Poor Quiyan fought pluckily, but his claws and teeth made little impression on the hard scaly body of his foe. In a few minutes he lay limp and still, a fat meal for the gluttonous victor.

JACK THE KOOKABURRA

PART I.

JACK, the Kookaburra, had for days been impatient to get out of his nest, which was in the spout of a grey gum tree, and to explore the big forest where his mother spent most of her time. He knew it must be jolly, for he often heard her and other members of the family laughing loudly. The sound was sometimes near at hand, but at other times, so far away that only a faint echo reached him. He was full fledged, and had discovered that he had a pair of fine wings, which he might flap to his enjoyment, if he only had room.

There had been three in the brood. One, a restless little thing, had been crowded out when three weeks old. Farmer Slocum, who lived near, had picked her up and put her in a wire cage so that no harm would come to her. He called her Goo-goo. The cage was hung under the verandah wall-plate, where the old birds came and fed the little prisoner, when no one was about.

The other had been a greater fidget, and a terrible squawk besides, and Jack chuckled to himself when the fledgling stood up at the entrance and toppled over.

He remembered the great row his parents kicked up when

they came home and saw a heap of feathers and a freshly severed beak on the grass. He had a livelier recollection of the whack on the ear he received for craning his neck round the doorpost. Then, when he was alone again, he had ventured to peep over the balcony to see what had become of little Johnny. At that instant, an enormous eagle lit almost on the front doorstep.

He gave a tremendous squawk, and backed in so precipitately, that his short tail feathers were crumpled up against the furniture. With his head bent low, and his neck stretched out, he peered affrightedly at the winged giant as long as he remained on the limb. He watched until the parents returned, when they ordered the intruder, in a loud voice, to get off the premises.

These things had made Jack more cautious. However, a hullabaloo at the next door neighbor's so worked on his curiosity that he could not restrain himself any longer. Out he scrambled on to the limb, where he made clumsy efforts to balance himself, while he took in the situation.

Far down the flat, he heard Pa Kookaburra laughing at the latest joke. Just behind him, where stood farmer Slocum's house, a quaint old dame was bustling through the grass towards a cackling hen. Directly in front of him, a pair of Bush Kingfishers were attacking a big goanna with all the fury and strength they were capable of.

They had pecked out a repository for their eggs in a white ants' nest, which was built high up on the trunk of a dead tree. Just under this nest, Kojurrie (the goanna) was clinging. He was waiting a favorable opportunity to steal the three or four pearly-white eggs within. His black head swung from side to side, and his forked tongue was darting in and out, as the excited birds flew and screeched at him. The Soldier Bird and the Magpie Lark came to help them, and their vicious smacks soon convinced him that an easier meal was to be got elsewhere.

As he scuttled away, the victorious kingfishers shook out their ruffled plumes, and talked at a great rate about the indignity, while Jack uttered a low chuckle of approval.

They were relations of his. Proud little beauties they were, in their showy collars. The female had a deep blue, and her mate a snow-white one. Compared with their brilliant colors, his own plumage was dull and commonplace. It varied from light chestnut to dusky brown on the back and wings, with dashes of shimmering blue on wings, shoulders, and lower portion of the back. The tail was brownish, barred, or mottled with black. There was a lot of white on the under parts, while the rest of his plumage was a light buff. The upper beak was brownish black; the under one, like the feet, was yellowish. He had also a sort of crest, noticeable when he was excited, or at such times when several were holding a corroboree.

He had other relatives, one of which, the Blue Kingfisher, haunted the rivers and creeks, and lived entirely on fish and aquatic insects. The Quatawur, (also called White-tail, Silver-tail, Racket-tail, and Cinnamon-breasted Kingfisher), was a northern beauty with a big red bill, blue crown, wings and tail. The latter was divided by two white central feathers which extended eight or nine inches beyond the others. The Quatawur laid three or four white eggs in an excavation made in the ground termites' nest. The Purple Kingfisher, and the Poditti, or Yellow-billed Kingfisher, a slaty-grey bird, with yellow and black on the head and back of the neck, were also relations. Another relative, the Sacred Kingfisher, a handsome blue and green bird whose screeching cree-cree-cree was already familiar to his ears, was a migrant who wintered in Northern Australia. This bird returned South in the spring, and laid four or five pinky-white eggs between October and December.

He had others, all more gaudy than himself, but, with the exception of the Kitticarrara, a beautiful bird with varying shades of blue on the wings and tail, who made a barking or yelping noise, and, who, like the Blue Kingfisher, plunged headlong after fish in the streams, they were all midgets in comparison. Some of his own species were prettily plumed in mottled chestnut. Others were snow-white, and white and chestnut, but the latter were more in the nature of freaks. He was the Great Brown Kingfisher, one of the bird oddities of the world, whose fame had spread to the farthest seas and the remotest lands.

He was feeling quite puffed up at this stage of his existence, for he was handsome in his sober way, and he had just mastered the art of reversing in one hop without tilting his tail over his back and welting the limb with his huge beak, when he descried a well-known form winging home across the plantation. He returned to the nest with all haste, and was waiting therein, like a dutiful boy, when his mother arrived and dropped a big worm into his capacious maw.

Before he was quite a month old, his mother allowed him to leave his retreat. Then commenced his flying lessons. The first step was a pretence. He would cling tightly to the limb while flapping mightily with his wings. After that, he took running hops along the limb, and flying hops to branches close by, followed by timid flutters to branches lower down.

In one of these flights, he missed his footing and fluttered to the ground. At this, the old birds made a tremendous row. They fluttered about in great excitement and ordered him to get aloft again. They flew down on the ground beside him, then flew up again, to show him how it was done. At the same time they koo-kooed and shouted to encourage him. But Jack put in a lot of practice on the ground before he succeeded in flapping laboriously up to the lowest branch. The old birds were soon beside him, and commemorated the event in a great laugh.

Next day he ventured on a flight to the nearest tree. He hit the limb clumsily, and had to flap desperately, as he hung on the side of it, to get his balance. But he was a proud little chap as he looked back, with his tail tilted up, and his neck and head feathers ruffled. Before the day waned, he had learned how to arrive without knocking the wind out of his body against the limb.

When his parents next left the roost, (soon after the Yellow Robin had announced the dawn, and while the Magpies were pouring out their rich melody), he flew off boldly with them, and endeavored, from a neighboring tree, to join in the salute to the summer morning. The effort was ludicrous, for the rollicking notes of his parents had not yet come to him, and would not for more than another month.

Within the house that stood near, Farmer Slocum was awakened by a dig in the ribs from his amiable spouse.

"There are the Jackasses, Bill!"

Bill at once got up and dressed. Like a good many more in the bush, his working day was from Jackass to Mopoke—a phrase which means from daylight to dusk. In earlier times, the Kookaburra was known as the "Settler's Clock," from a belief that his joyful paeans were vented regularly at morn, noon, and dusk. He was supposed to be silent through the heat of the forenoon, and the wane of the afternoon. But the Kookaburra laughed just when the fit took him, particularly when excited. This excitement occurred at any hour during the day. He would laugh as readily at the violent death of his mother-in-law, as he would at the enraged settler when he fell off his haystack. When one alighted alone in a tree from a fairly long flight, he would generally laugh loudly, and repeat at intervals until joined by a mate. A bird in one tree would also answer a brother in a neighboring tree. The refrain would be caught up by others in the distance, in the same manner as cockerels answer one another at night. Again, when two came together on a limb, their mutual greeting was boisterous, and, when several met from different directions, it was unanimously accepted as an occasion for general rejoicing.

When Slocum got down to his ploughing, the birds were

already waiting for him on a stump. He had long been accustomed to the two old birds.

Still, he could not tell at a little distance that the third was a young one, for the only difference in their appearances was that the adults were a little darker on the backs and wings. Careful measurement might have shown a little difference in size. The adult length was eighteen inches, and included five-and-a-half inch tail, and three inch bill. When they continued to feed him in the open, and when he did not take part in their rejoicings, of course, his youthfulness was betrayed.

They flew to the furrow when the plough started, and followed along behind, picking up the white grubs, toads, frogs, beetles, and worms. To get a meal there was easy, and ere many days Jack was killing his own grubs and snails by battering them against the clods. Now and again, the farmer turned up a nest of young mice, with the remark that it was "a feast for the Jackasses."

Slocum always called them jackasses. He also called his wife a jackass when she took a silly fit of giggling. The name probably originated from jacasse, the French word for kingfisher, though there were several versions as to the derivation. One bush version was that the cry in the distance was mistaken for the bray of an ass by a newchum named Jack. His mates afterwards so mercilessly chaffed him about his ass that the bird became generally known as "Jack's Ass." Another had an aboriginal origin. A blackfellow, struck by some resemblance in a hilarious miner to the laughing bird, called him "chaka-chaka." The miners subsequently alluded to the birds as Chaka-Chakas. This was soon shortened to Chakas, and that in turn corrupted to Jackass. Still another yarn had it that an early immigrant, on being told by a scientific person that the name of the bird was Dacelo gigas, interpreted thus to his mates: "He says 'that's an ol' jackass.' "

One day, Slocum, finding a squirming snake thrust through the wires of the cage on the verandah, remarked that it was time

Goo-goo was liberated. So he took her down the farm, and, after exercising her wings by throwing her up in the air a few times, left her with the old birds, who greeted her return with exultant notes.

PART II.

On Sundays, and occasionally on other days when the ploughman did not turn up as usual, they would linger for hours about the ground, waiting for their breakfast to be unearthed. Now and again, they would relieve their feelings in a noisy duet. Finally, they would fly across the hills and flats in quest of caterpillars, small lizards and snakes, or even grasshoppers. On one of these jaunts, Jack discovered a carpet snake coiled, roll upon roll, round its big cluster of eggs, which it was hatching. In a ferment of excitement, he darted for the nearest branch, and made the bush ring with his cries. He was three months old then, and could make as much clatter as Mrs. Slocum. In his own way he was calling to Dad Kookaburra: "Quick! here's a snake. Koo-o! a whopper."

The parents came, saw the coiled monster, and set up a cackle that brought a score more of the family hurrying to the scene. These became equally excited, and made an echoing guffaw that was repeated again and again. But none of them attempted to disturb the python. Jack soon learnt that it was not wise to attack big snakes, which included the adult black, brown and the death adder, though he might jeer at them to his heart's content. He could not swallow them if he did kill them, and Jack was a wise bird who killed only what he could eat.

He had often killed and eaten blind snakes, which had been

turned up by the ploughshare, but it was not till the following spring that he had his first encounter with a reptile in the open forest. It was a whip snake, which he found in a bush. He did not attack it immediately, but flew to an adjacent limb, from which coign of vantage he eyed it critically. Then he threw up his head, and with his big mandibles wide apart, his closed wings moving in little flutters against his side, announced hysterically that the wonderful snake killing act was about to commence. This over, he gazed down with a quaint aspect of apathy and reflection. When the snake moved, he craned forward with a steely glint in his dark brown eyes. He made presently a swift feint at the bush, and uttered a low fierce koo-koo-ka as he passed it. Wheeling, he fluttered over it. Still chattering, he returned to his perch, and again uttered his noisy paean.

This paean was continued at intervals until he was joined by another Kookaburra. The snake had meanwhile slid to the ground. As soon as it had crawled clear of the bush, he made a bold sweep on to it, and chopped it with a wrenching movement across the neck. As he circled back to his perch, the snake squirmed violently in the grass. In a moment he was down again, and this time he lifted it above the tree tops, and then dropped it. As it neared the ground the other bird darted out suddenly and caught it, and carried it high into the air, when it was again dropped. Then Jack swooped down and caught it. This was repeated several times. On each occasion, the birds rose with a heavy fluttering motion of the wings, with the beak pointed downwards, to guard against the doubling movements of the victim.

After a while, one of them carried it to a limb, and the other joined him with a triumphant laugh. Then commenced a lively tug-of-war. One moment, the snake, perceptibly stretching, would be hanging over the limb, with a bird hanging under each side with closed wings. One would presently let go, and the other,

(Lawrence & Littlejohns.)
JACK, THE KOOKABURRA.

A GROUP OF KOOKABURRAS. *(A.J. Campbell)*

with a startled squawk, would fall with a sudden recoil of the snake. The tussle was renewed on the ground, then again in the air, and once more on the limb. At times, one would be clinging desperately to the perch, holding the neck of the reptile, while the other would hang beneath with a bulldog grip on the tail.

A dozen more Kookaburras had now arrived, and the forest resounded with their levity. The contestants hung on grimly until another bird darted in between, and, getting a central grip on the green streak, mixed them all up in a squabbling heap. When the prey was dropped, a fourth bird swooped down and caught it.

So the tussle and the row went on, now among the branches, or in the air, now on the ground, till finally Jack emerged from the grass with the prize half swallowed, and, with the other half hanging out of his gaping beak, flew heavily away to finish his meal.

It took him half-an-hour to get it all down. For a considerable time he remained in a sleepy state, and looked very uncomfortable. Jack, however, was provided with a quick-acting powerful digestive apparatus, so much so that one end of his meal was already in process of digestion while the other end was swallowed.

Towards sunset he was feeling sprightly again. Then he recollected that he had seen a pretty little lady Kookaburra among the attendance at the scrimmage, and he was prompted to become acquainted with her without delay.

He had not long to look for her, for it was the hour when Kookaburras were particularly merry. Guided by the voices, he was soon beside her, and introduced himself with a gurgling laugh that dinned in her ears. Then, sidling up to her, he touched the point of her beak with the tip of his, and laughed again. This time she joined him. Then they reversed, and had another laugh. Their courtship, if short, was a most hilarious affair. When he was not loudly proclaiming his joy, he was chuckling to her, or making demonstrations in dumb show as if he were persuading her to elope with him.

The night found them roosting together in an ironbark tree on a stony ridge.

Now commenced the important preparations for nesting. There was no difficulty in finding a suitable place, for drooping spouts, which they dearly loved, were plentiful. But there was a tree-ants' nest as well near the spot, and the trouble was to decide which to have. The ants' nest was ultimately favored. The surface was almost as hard as cement. Unable to make any impression on it, Jack, after exhaustive prospecting, flew off some distance, and, wheeling about, rushed at it with such force that the grit whizzed from the blow of the wonderful beak. Having cracked the surface, the bird proceeded with the excavation of the nest. Both took part in the work, and continued patiently and tirelessly until the required dimensions were attained. The swarming termites within, shrinking from the light, at once blocked up the passages leading into the chamber. In such nests it was not uncommon to see termites crawling among the eggs or young birds. If the nest was considerably disturbed, the rightful owners sometimes abandoned it.

Early in September, four beautiful pearl-white eggs were placed in the snug nest. They were one-and-three-quarter inches long by one-and-half inches broad. This size was a shade bigger than the eggs of the white cockatoo. During the period of incubation, Jack was never far away, and encouraged his mate with his cheery cackle many times between sunrise and sunset.

When the chicks appeared, he played no small part in providing for them. They were hungry, clamorous little things, that never seemed satisfied, and leapt noisily forward with their capacious mouths wide open when any bird whatsoever fluttered within hearing. At times, Jack would look meditatively into the nest as if disgusted with his gluttonous progeny. However, in echoing shouts from the tree-tops, he would presently let the general public know that he was still happy, though married.

There were other busy couples in the neighborhood. Most of their nests were in hollow spouts, some high and some low, and none of them lined in any way. The eggs rested on the dust of decayed wood. His sister Goo-goo was not one of these. She nested late in the season, and produced only one clutch.

Having few natural enemies, and being treated as almost sacred by most bushmen, his species might have become numerous throughout the broad gum forests of the east. He feared neither hawk nor eagle, and only at night did he dread the spotted sneak, Buckandee, or Native Cat, and the Bushy-tailed Rat, which occasionally managed to steal upon birds as they slept on their perches. But there were men who exercised no forbearance towards them. Gadney, who was Slocum's neighbor, was one of these. His method was to cripple one, and the terrific row that would be raised by the wounded bird would bring all others within hearing into the nearest trees. He would then continue the slaughter as long as any remained within gunshot.

"You ought to get six months," said Slocum, hotly, as he rode up on one occasion. "Those birds are not only harmless, but do good in killing vermin."

"What about killing chickens!" demanded Gadney. "That fellow there had a chicken in his mouth when I potted him."

"It's very rarely a Jackass interferes with chickens, Gadney," said Slocum. "And if an odd one does get tempted to act in that way, it's no reason why you should clear the whole bush of them. Most people in this country want them to live, and you've got no right to destroy what the people have a national claim to."

Many a brood, orphaned by Gadney's gun, died miserably of starvation in their nests. Others escaped only to fall into the hands of professional bird-catchers. Being attractive, the poor birds were much sought after, and everywhere nests were robbed for metropolitan and foreign markets.

The thieves appeared on the stony ridge when the babies in

the ants' nest were still unshapely forms with sprouting tails. They would halt near by, their van laden with boxes covered with wire-netting, in which were birds of many kinds. Among them were several young kookaburras, who fed ravenously on the fresh meat that was thrust through the meshes.

Having a prying, inquisitive nature, Jack perched himself in a convenient position to watch. Nothing escaped his keen eye. The kindling of the fire to boil the men's billy especially interested him. The appearance of smoke, in fact, was an occasion for jubilation. When they attempted to climb his nest tree, however, his feathered bosom swelled with resentment. His daring in defence of the young provoked the men to throw sticks and other missiles at him. Still, when they were off their guard, he darted savagely at them, and his strong beak snapped loudly near their heads. His mate was equally excited and aggressive, and uttered a low, angry chatter, that was like a growl, as she swooped past. The ladder was luckily not long enough, and, as there were no secure limbs within reach over which to throw a rope, they at last departed. The echoing notes of the jubilant couple rang in their ears as they went.

It was just about six weeks after the eggs were laid that the little ones left the nest and learnt to fly. In November, the mother commenced to lay again. The same nest was used, for it had not been vacated long enough for the industrious termites to fill up the excavation. Whether they filled it in or not subsequently, there was not much probability that Jack would be found again carrying on business at the old address. His mother was breeding that year in the old spout where he was hatched, but most of her comrades had sought new quarters.

When the second brood were finally dismissed, there followed a long period of comparative quiescence, until the breeding season came round again. Besides the joys of hatching and rearing the young ones, spring and summer brought thrilling snake adventures, and the excitement of bush fires. A smoke-cloud attracted them as well as the hawks and kites. Whereas the hawks soared high in the air, Jack and his kin flew from tree to tree as the fire advanced, and watched the ground closely for retreating vermin. Burning brush and burning logs were also watched, sometimes for several hours at a stretch.

It was near a brush fire that he had his most memorable adventure. He had tackled a half-grown diamond snake, which, with a lightning movement, threw its coils around him. For a moment he was in a sorry predicament, and screeched in terror as the coils tightened. His companions, flocking about him, were tumultuous in their excitement. When it seemed that the life would be crushed out of him, one, with a vicious snap, broke the reptile's neck, and the coils relaxed. Jack took no part in the subsequent proceedings. He was too busy shaking himself and wiping his bill on a stump.

Still he was not daunted. Ere a week had elapsed, he attacked a brown snake on the open flat. The brown was a venomous reptile, and quick in its movements. He did not fear its fangs so much as its coils, for his thick coat of feathers protected his body. He was alone. The snake's head was raised to strike as he approached it warily on the ground. For awhile they sparred for an opening. The snake led with a vicious lunge, and was instantly knocked flat with a sharp smack of the strong wing, which was thrown out as the bird dodged aside. It was slightly dazed, but more savage as it raised its head again. There was more sparring, more lunging and dodging, and Jack scored an occasional dig with his beak between whiles. The snake fought gamely, but soon the set curves of its body gave way to a hopeless wriggle. Jumping in quickly, he dealt the knockout blow with his bill on the neck.

After a few minutes, he carried it high into the air, and let it drop over a clear patch. As it fell with violence, he followed it down, and picked it up again from the ground. Twice he repeated this performance before he commenced leisurely to swallow the limp and battered victim.

Though he loved the open forests, and very seldom drank, even in the summer months, he went down to the river now and again for a change of diet. Here he would plunge into the water after yabbies, and would sometimes go right under. He gathered mussels, too, in the shallows along the edge. When he got one, he carried it to a log and whacked it thereon repeatedly until it opened.

Between whiles, he perched on a dry limb, and watched the more expert fishing of his small relative, the Blue Kingfisher, whose nest was tunnelled, a foot deep, into the broken bank. If one examined that domicile about October or December, he would find six or seven baby birds, and a quantity of fish bones and remnants of water beetles all mixed up together. When he was not bringing in more fish, or quietly watching from a projecting snag, the saucy little male was shooting like a blue meteor up and down stream in pursuit of a brother. Sometimes, he flew with a screech at Jack, for any intrusion whatever he resented at breeding time. Jack merely opened his mouth and said "Yah!" as the little spitfire shot past.

Summer and winter he stuck to his native district. His wanderings in quest of food covered a radius of only a few miles. His flights were never long. He flew low and not very fast. Sometimes, he perched on the telegraph wire by the railway line, and looked down unconcernedly at the passing train. At other times, he would alight on a roof in the township, and surprise newcomers with his cachinnations.

His favorite perches were on Slocum's barn, and on the gallows at the slaughter yard, though he looked disdainfully on the offal and carrion which the Crows and the Kurrawongs (Pied Bell Magpies) liked so much.

Many a time he had seen the rabbit poisoner drive through the station paddocks that lay beyond, but he did not know that this person was the cause of the heavy mortality he had noticed everywhere among the birds.

One April day, when he was hungry and listless, he picked up a bait that had been dropped among the stones, on the ridge. Perhaps he mistook it for a grub or a beetle. Certainly he beat it on the ground several times before he swallowed it. Shortly afterwards, he was threshing around in agony, while his comrades cackled loudly overhead.

A little later, while gathering wood, Slocum found his dead body under a bush.

"The squatters have done for you, Jack, with their plaguy phosphorus," he said as he turned the bird over tenderly with his foot. "And you never did them any harm."

Warrigal the Dingo

PART I.

WARRIGAL'S home was a big log in a luxuriant New England valley. In its dark hollow the atmosphere was stuffy and the odor vile. Outside, the mid-October days were cool and sweet.

His eyes had not long opened, and he was still curiously looking at the five other pups that sprawled around him. In front, with her forepaws out, crouched his mother, who watched the entrance.

She suddenly half rose, and he saw her body quiver, then set as if for a spring. He knew instinctively that some danger was at hand. Squatting on his haunches he looked out, and framed in the circle of light was a strange face—his first glimpse of man.

The overseer of Barney Downs had noticed the little pad leading to the log. A quantity of bones and feathers, dead lambs and small marsupials, at the entrance told him the nature of the occupants. When he saw the green gleam of the mother's eyes in the gloom, he was pleased.

The Stock Protection Board paid him a pound each for the scalps, by which means he added considerably to his year's wages.

"I'll be out here with an axe first thing tomorrow," he remarked, and dropping a poisoned bait in a tussock of grass, he rode away.

For an hour the mother Dingo did not move. She then cautiously crept out and scented all round where he had been. She pawed the bait suspiciously, and smelt it. It was a dainty piece of fresh meat, which he had been careful not to handle. He had placed the strychnine in a small incision with a knife, and wrapped the bait in a sheet of clean paper. But her natural cunning matched the acquired cunning of the man. Further, she knew it was not safe to remain there now that her den had been discovered.

At dusk, she seized Warrigal by the scruff of the neck, and carried him to another log, two miles away, that was screened with deep grass and fern. Five more trips she made. When all were safe in their new home, she went out into the night to hold council with the pack, and to seek food for her pups.

In the evenings when the mother was present, they sat or played at the mouth of the log. During these times, Warrigal saw many of the pack that haunted that locality. They were of several colors—tan, brindle, and black predominating—the result of intermingling with tame dogs of camp and squattage, and admitting into the brotherhood the renegades of bush towns. Though the average domestic animal would do his utmost to kill the wild dog, if set on and followed, he was just as likely, if left alone, to rub noses and enter into a compact to go bushranging together. Many a high-class dog, whose character had hitherto been irreproachable, had been led astray by a dingo mate, and many a tame female dog had been stolen by the denizens of the wild.

Warrigal had been there a week when the overseer again discovered his retreat. In a moment he was chopping at the log with his tomahawk.

He had forgotten to block the exit, and, at the first blow, the mother dashed out and bolted into the bush, leaving her progeny to take care of themselves.

"That's a good scalp I've lost," the overseer grumbled; "she'll very likely go right away, and never return even for tidings of her pups."

One by one he dragged the pups out and killed them. Warrigal, cowering in the farthest corner, was the last to be hauled through the aperture. He was a fine big fellow, a true dingo, reddish-yellow to reddish-brown in color, with pricked ears and bushy tail.

The overseer looked him over with admiration, and, reflecting that many stockowners used the dingo for crossing purposes on account of his sagacity and skill at shepherding, he decided to spare him.

He carried him home on the pommel of the saddle. Warrigal on the way made many desperate but futile attempts to jump to the ground. When his mother had carried him in her teeth he did not move, but this was a weird and terrifying experience that he could not understand.

When he was set down at the homestead, he darted under the house, from which it took one of the station children half-an-hour to recover him. He crouched under chairs, under the table—under any cover that was available.

The children made a pet of him, and, finding they were friends, he lost his timidity.

Very early, he assumed the office of watch dog, to the disgust of old Jack, the sheep dog, who was often asleep on the shady side of the house.

Nothing escaped his notice Whenever he saw his associates engaged in anything that was new to him, he brought a studious eye to bear upon it as though there was nothing in the world he desired more to learn than that particular business.

In a few months, he knew the language of fowls, and required no telling to "look out" when an enemy was around. He followed and yelped at a hawk that was a mere speck in the atmosphere. He put the ducks into their house every evening, and, if a hen was pecking about after sunset, he wanted to know why.

He slept just outside the overseer's door, which was left ajar in warm weather. In the morning, as soon as the bell rang, he slipped into the room, and plainly indicated to the overseer that it was time to get up. If he found him asleep, he stood on his hind legs and tapped him gently on the chest with his paw until he waked him. Then he wagged his tail and panted with delight.

Though the little ones played roughly with him, rode on his back and pulled his tail, he never attempted to bite. As he had played with his own kin, so he played with them. They were nearer to the primitive than the grown-ups. He took no indignities from the station hands. His gleaming white teeth were bared as a hint when they had gone far enough. No strange dogs came to the place unchallenged, nor did the station dogs take liberties with him when he had grown big and strong.

Old Jack, who had bossed the kennel for years, rushed at him one morning as they were feeding by the kitchen. The unexpected jolt nearly knocked him off his feet. Snarling and bristling, he turned upon the aggressor.

His mode of attack differed from that of all other dogs. He dodged the rush of his antagonist, and with a quick sweeping snap laid his shoulder open. Stung and bleeding, Jack sprang for the throat, but Warrigal shot past him with his head low, and took a piece clean out as he went. Several times the manoeuvre was repeated, with short savage bouts and clashing of fangs between. The old dog attacked with head high, and stood above his adversary, who crouched and sidestepped, silent and watchful.

Warrigal took what bites he got without a whimper. He darted in without a growl. His swift, half-gliding, elusive spring puzzled his foe. The latter fought with ferocity, whilst Warrigal exhibited no temper, except in the suggested savagery of his bared fangs as he met the other's fierce onslaughts. Once the old dog got a grip on his neck. Then Warrigal's jaws snapped like a steel trap on his foreleg. As he limped back on three legs, whimpering, Warrigal darted in and caught him by the throat.

Down and over he went, with the sharp teeth sinking deeply, and the blood reddening his muzzle.

The cook, who had watched the battle with great interest, now grabbed a broom and drove him away.

From that time there was a change in Warrigal. Not that he was aggressive or domineering. He was as peaceful and tractable as ever, but he was restless and discontented. Towards nightfall he sat in front of the house, listening intently and looking out into the bush. Now and again he threw back his head and uttered the wild cry of his fathers. He had picked up an imitation bark from the squatter's dogs, though he seldom used it. His signal call was a sharp, snappish yelp, and a short howl that broke suddenly on the night air, and died away to nothing, with a far-away sound that lingered in the ear. It could be heard at a greater distance than the much noisier howl of the domestic dog. It was a dismal sort of howl, yet with nothing of melancholy in it. It simply filled one with a sense of utter loneliness.

One night, he trotted down the slope into a little gully. There he sat awhile and looked back, debating whether he would remain with man or return to his own. Then he gave a long howl and went on down the gully and out into the broad bush. Soon he met a wild brother, foraging in company with a female of the species. The latter he chummed with, and, if there had been any liklihood before of his returning to the homestead, there was none now. His native wilds had reclaimed him.

Strong, vigorous, and full of the joy of living, he romped with her under the fragrant trees, and rolled delightfully on the grass. He sniffed the delicious scent of the forest, while the cry of the night-birds stirred him like the remembrance of some half-forgotten dream. A handsome, well-set animal, he bore himself ever with pride and gracefulness. Not only did he belong to the higher order of animals—not only was his species the highest type of Australian animal—but he represented the only true

(A. H. Mattingley.)

WARRIGAL, THE DINGO.

A Dingo in Captivity (Melbourne Zoo).

(W. H. D. Le Souef)

wild dog in the world. His sign of distinction was three pairs of molars in the lower jaw, whereas all Asiatic breeds had only two.

Towards morning, a drizzling rain drove them to seek shelter. Mirri, his companion, led the way to a cave in a secluded gorge. Her former consort was already there. As it was a large cave, Warrigal did not disturb him, but coiled up with his mate in another corner.

They did not sleep there all day, but hunted irregularly by day or night. They, however, made the cave their home. There were wild dogs everywhere in the bush. They were distributed over all Australia. With the exception of those in the dry interior, who made burrows in the sandhills in a somewhat similar manner to the Wombat, and followed the watercourses from one sheep run to another after heavy rains, each pack kept always to its native beat, unless driven afield by hunters. They usually roamed about singly or in pairs, and only occasionally formed into packs.

Warrigal's first introduction to the pack was at night, when a noisy concert was held on a cattle-camp. Afterwards, they rounded up a mob of sheep, and, working like trained sheep dogs, drove them along a creek to a fence. Here the majority held them, whilst Warrigal and three others went into the mob at different points to kill a sheep to serve as a banquet for the pack.

They did not kill for killing's sake. Unlike the half-breed, who would tear and mangle a score of sheep just for amusement, they left no torn ones behind them if they could help it. The half-breed would kill lambs and bury them for future use, and he was not averse to high-flavored carcases lying about the bush when hungry. He would also carry home a bone that had no substance in it, and hide it for gnawing purposes. Such habits were foreign to the pure native.

Each of the three harmed but one sheep, and that one he killed outright. Nor was it in all cases the first he came to. He beat about until he found a hogget fat and tempting enough to suit him. He was extremely partial to lambs.

As the sheep gave him little chance to make a good selection in the open, experience had taught him to follow or drive them to a corner, where he could choose at his leisure. If in urgent need of a meal, at the time, however, he would dive straight in and lay hold of the first mutton available.

When they had made their kills, the rest of the mob was allowed to go.

The overseer, who blamed the wild dogs for taking Warrigal away, came upon the remains of the carcases a few days later, and determined to use every artifice he knew to capture their scalps. Warrigal, who had jumped up on a high log to take a careful survey of his surroundings, as the land thereabouts was low and deeply grassed, saw his former master pass along towards a boundary-rider's hut at the back of the run. He had a good eye, and discerned objects at a great distance. Jumping down, he loped along to the horse's track, which he followed for more than a mile. But he had no idea of returning, or of venturing near the hut. Perhaps it was well he did not do so, for the overseer heard more about the doings of the dingoes on his arrival there.

Only that morning the boundary-rider had surprised two dingoes droving in the adjoining paddock.

"One," he said, "was a big yellow brute; the other was smaller with dark splashes about him. They had lifted about two hundred ewes, and were jogging along all serene, though a bit short-handed. The big fellow seemed to be boss. When a sheep broke out, the little chap, keeping wide, would lope leisurely after it, and look back over his shoulder at the big chap. The big chap would stand and watch him. If he fiddled about much, he would sit down and pant like fury. By and bye he would get up and fidget round, then squat down again and swear. 'Hang it all, Brindle,' he would growl, 'chuck yourself round a bit, or we shall be here all day.' You could see it bristling out of him. It was pretty sultry weather just then, and I think Brindle, being the rouseabout, had done most of the rounding up and steadying at the start, and was too tired to care if he got the sack. They were not saying a word to the sheep, but just trotting to and fro, and keeping a look-out for trouble. I was on the point of riding out and demanding the way bill, when the boss spotted me in the timber. He propped short, shut his mouth up suddenly and stared, 'Well, dinner's off!' he said, looking disgustedly at Brindle. Then he lit out for next week without giving delivery."

"Have you seen anything of Warrigal?" asked the overseer.

"I believe I saw him yesterday," the boundary-rider replied. "If it wasn't him it was his double. He and another dog were dodging round a cow and calf, and nipping the young one whenever they got a chance. After a bit one got in front to draw the cow, and as soon as she charged, the other darted between and cut off the calf. Five other dogs, that had been lying low for that opportunity, then sprang up and surrounded it. They worked like dogs that had been trained for the show—blocking it promptly when it tried to break in any direction but the way they wanted to drive it. They were all cool and calculating; and none of them uttered a sound. The old cow let out a frantic bellow, and came running back. Three dogs tried to block her, while two others made desperate efforts to kill the calf. One had gripped it by the flank, another by the throat, and they had almost got it to the ground when the cow rushed through and rescued it. Five of them drew aside as before, and the remaining pair started their dodging tactics over again. At that stage, I arrived on the scene with a great clatter and a loud yell. Six of the calf-hunters made a dash for the scrub at once. The other one, which I think was Warrigal, stood for a moment and wagged his tail, as if he had a mind to stop and renew old acquaintance. Then he seemed to remember suddenly that he had more urgent affairs to attend to elsewhere, and he got to that scrub quicker than any of them."

PART II.

Soon after this, Warrigal saw traces everywhere that the hunters were at work. Baits wrapped in paper were dropped into tussocks and bushes along the gullies and creeks where he loved to ramble. Poisoned bones were hung over fences and low limbs with copper wire. Here and there, a strong line with a baited hook was hung in a similar way. Following a trail that had been drawn with the fresh paunch of a bullock, he came upon a luckless hybrid who was caught by the paw in a steel trap. The trap had been carefully buried on the trail, and a dog's paw had been used to scrape over it. The hybrid, having scented this, thought he had struck the plant of one of his fellows, and with a grin on his countenance started to scratch. The next instant there was a terrifying snap, and the steel teeth held him fast.

Warrigal circled round him a couple of times with raised bristles and excited eyes. He well knew that this was the work of man. Indeed, his nostrils, sniffing quickly over the ground, easily picked up the scent. It was old, but he was wise, and, springing on to a stump, he looked carefully over the landscape before he resumed his investigations along the trail.

There were other traps cunningly hidden on the way, but he avoided them all. At the end of the trail, he found the paunch, which had been poisoned and left on a favorite beat. He merely smelt it and passed on. Like the black, he was a smart tracker.

He noticed the broken twig, the crushed blade of grass, and the disturbed pebble, even though he had not yet struck the scent. He had also a sharp ear, a keen sense of smell, and a delicate palate. His need of food would be very pressing before he would touch the daintiest piece of fresh meat that had been handled by man.

Being a clean and cunning animal, he much preferred to kill his own meat, and, where it was plentiful, he killed at least once a day, mostly about sunset. He returned to his quarry early next morning for breakfast, after which he never touched it again.

The biting New England winter was over the land. The frost-coated grass crackled underfoot, and the icicles, hanging from the trees, glistened in the morning sun. It was a bad time for the wild dogs, who were cold and hungry.

One evening, while loping along the foot of a ridge, Warrigal was astonished to see a little girl standing with her back to a tree. She held a long stick in her hands, whilst close in front of her were six dingoes, watching her with greedy eyes. She was a selector's daughter, who had wandered away and was lost.

Remembering the children who had played with him in his young days at Barney Downs, Warrigal trotted up to them. Bristling from head to tail, snarling and gnashing his teeth, he drove back his savage kindred. Then he ran up to the little girl, wagged his tail, sat up, held out his paw and made it clear in a dog's way that he was a friend. She understood, and welcomed him as a protector.

She tied her handkerchief round his neck to hold him near her. She did not now fear the dingoes, but she was trembling with cold. As night came on, she led him under a thick bush, and when he lay down she snuggled up to him for warmth. In that position, with her hand grasping the improvised collar, sleeping and waking, she passed the lonely night.

The sun was peeping over the ridge, when the searchers, who had camped on the girl's tracks, discovered her. In her joy, she let the dog go and ran to meet her father. A few moments later, when she looked back for her brute companion, he had disappeared.

Warrigal was making good progress towards a patch of thick scrub he knew, where he intended to camp till evening. On the way, he came upon a small flock of sheep, which suggested breakfast. He was ravenously hungry, but for all that he hesitated to follow them as they ran off.

"I'll have a look about first," he thought, and jumped up on to a stump.

The overseer, going out early to join the searchers, observed the disturbed flock, and pulled up in a little clump of bushes just as Warrigal leaped on the stump.

"I've got you now, you rascal!" said the overseer, who was armed with a rifle.

Holding the reins in the crook of his arm, he slewed in the saddle and fired. The dog, however, had seen the glint of the lifting barrel, and the bullet merely chipped the skin of his bristling neck as he dropped down.

With protruding eyes and dripping jaws, he dashed away at his utmost speed, nor once looked back until he had gained the shelter of the scrub.

Striking another trail, which had been made with aniseed, he ran it out at a concealed pit in an old cattle-yard. The pit was covered with a heavy swing lid, which was very evenly balanced on a centre axle. The aniseed was trailed across it, and, as a further lure, a dog had been short-chained on it. With his nose to the ground, he explored the whole yard. He had some doubts about the trapdoor, but he had walked on boards many a time, and, being interested in the scent, he stepped on to it. There was no time to get back. It swung under his weight, and, struggling desperately, he dropped into the pit.

No dog was ever more disgusted. When he realised that he

was a prisoner, rage more than fear possessed him. He walked round and round the pit, scratching here and there, and trying to scale the steep sides. Now and again, he stood on his hind legs and whined at the light above. With the fall of night, he changed his tune to a despairing howl.

In the morning, the boundary-rider came and lifted the lid. Warrigal's heart had thumped with fear when he heard the approaching footsteps, but, at sight of the bearded face of his one-time friend, he took courage. He assumed a most affectionate manner, wagged his tail expressively, and made the best attempt he could at a friendly bark.

"Why, bless me if it isn't Warrigal!" said the surprised boundary-rider. "Well, well! To think that you'd fall in, when half the wild dogs are too cute to be caught in such a trap. Wonder now if you'll give up your bad habits and be a respectable, civilised dog, you villain, if I take you home. . . . I'll chance it, anyway."

He lifted him out, and Warrigal danced and capered around him with exuberant joy.

"Come here, you scamp!" said his rescuer, seating himself on a post lying in the yard.

"Sit up!"

The dog sat straight up, as he had been taught at the squattage.

"Shake hands!"

He held out his paw immediately.

"You haven't forgotten your table manners, you scamp. I think you'll follow me home now."

He patted him, then mounted his horse.

Warrigal followed him as though he was delighted to have a master again.

He followed him for two miles, then he espied a kangaroo hopping leisurely over a low hill, and at once he dashed away in pursuit. The boundary-rider galloped after him, anxiously calling to him to come back, but Warrigal wanted breakfast. He saw it in front of him, for though he killed sheep when he was hungry, and they were handy, he lived principally on marsupials, which had been the food of his race for unknown centuries.

In the rough, thickly-timbered country, the boundary-rider soon lost sight of him, and, greatly disappointed, gave up the chase.

Over flats and ridges, across creeks and gullies, and down long winding hollows, Warrigal pursued his prey. Being in the habit of using his brains and saving his legs, he was not swift. At the start the kangaroo was fleeter, dashing away from him in quick spurts; but he had more stamina. He was patient and persevering—a hunter of no mean skill. Though, at times, a long way behind his quarry, he bounded along on the scent at an even pace, determined and confident of success. His steady, swinging gallop gradually wore down the marsupial, and, on a clear spot, putting on a spurt for the first time, he drew up and caught him by the tail. With a sharp twist, he threw the big animal, then sprang to the head and drove his teeth in behind the ears.

After drinking and cooling himself in a water-hole near by, he ate his fill of the warm meat, and returned to his den in the cave.

"The next time you get hold of him," said the overseer, on learning of the morning's adventure, "give him a bullet."

Sheep continued to be killed on the run, and Warrigal was blamed, unjustly, for most of the mischief. Other dogs as persistently avoided baits and traps, and eluded capture by the craftiest methods that could be devised. Warrigal, however, being individually known, acquired a notoriety that no wise dog would have envied. The reward offered for his scalp steadily rose until, by the time he was three years old, it had mounted to ten guineas. Several selectors, who also had lost sheep, subscribed half the amount.

The selectors knew him well, and, when one of them saw him while kangaroo-hunting with three half-bred greyhounds, he gave eager chase. Warrigal sped through a wire fence into a thick scrub, where the selector could not follow. The greyhounds, however, kept after him, and, overtaking him in a deep gorge, all three pounced savagely upon him. He fought fiercely for a little while, just long enough to realise that he had no chance against them. Only by strategy could he escape with his life. Being bowled over, and unable to rise again, he let his head drop suddenly and feigned death. Silently, and without flinching, he bore the punishment of tearing claw and rending fang.

Finding him limp and apparently lifeless, they desisted, and presently left him. He did not move, and scarcely breathed, until he could no longer hear them.

He cautiously raised his head and looked about him, and then staggered to his feet and limped painfully away down the gorge. He was frightfully injured, and his coat was soaked with blood that streamed from many gaping wounds.

Stiff and weak, he reached the cave, where he lay a helpless cripple for more than a week. Mirri, who had led him there in the wet night long ago, was affectionately concerned about his condition. He had not taken much notice of her of late, but now she stood between him and the shadow of death. In her dark corner were five little pups. He lay near them, and shared the food which the mother brought for them.

When he could get about again, he contented himself for a time with catching possums. This did not require a great deal of exertion. He cunningly waited in the long grass, and, when a possum came down to the ground, he darted between it and the tree. He caught hares and rabbits in plenty, and prowled stealthily through the grass in quest of pottoroos. Regaining his old vigor, he rambled again over distant beats, sometimes alone, and sometimes in company.

One day, the overseer had been riding in a hollow near by, and, hearing a howl, he drew his stirrup and bore down at full gallop. He was quickly alongside the scared dingo, but the horse being a young one, swerved sharply whenever he felt the stirrup. Warrigal was headed for a patch of brushwood, and, when the overseer rode in front, he kept straight after him, determined not to be turned off a bee-line course to that brush. The overseer's older horses were trained to gallop on to a dingo and strike him down with their forefeet. When he tried to ride over Warrigal with this colt, it took exceptional pains not to tread on him, and he reached his haven of refuge without injury.

When he joined his fellows, the pack led off to a waterhole, and, shortly after drinking, two fell down and commenced to struggle violently. They had killed a sheep that morning, and at sunset had returned for the second feast. In the meantime, the boundary-rider had craftily poisoned the carcase. The other dingoes formed a ring around the victims, and watched the death throes with fear in their hearts. When the struggles ceased, they slunk away, uttering mournful howls at intervals as they scattered about the bush.

Picking up his old mate in the evening, he led her away from the abodes of man to the foot-hills of a rugged range, where he crouched in the gloom of a cavern by day, and from whence he emerged only under cover of night. In that virgin haunt, restraint came rarely to the promptings of his untamable blood, and in all his glory he trod with velvet paws through gorge and gully, and followed lone pads that countless wild beasts had trodden through æons of time.

Bluey the Wren.

PART I.

THE BLUE WREN was a helpless, naked mite, with tightly-sealed eyelids, when young Bob Bucknell discovered him in a cosy dome-shaped nest of grass, hidden low down in a thorny bush.

Bob was a selector's son, a barefooted urchin who spent all his spare time wandering about the bush, and along the banks of the river and creeks. He was a nature lover of the impish variety. He would not destroy an egg, neither would he damage a nest, but he played tricks on the birds. For instance, he would put the Redbreast's eggs into the nest of the Native Canary, and the latter's eggs into the Redbreast's nest. His interest in the result, when the young birds were fledged, was so absorbent that he often went without his meals to watch them. Many of his experiments were successful, and at the same time amusing to himself. But there were birds, such as the Swallow, Willy Wagtail, and Lyre Bird, which could not be imposed upon, nor would they tolerate any interference with their domestic arrangements. The last named would abandon her nest if the egg was only touched by hand. The Willy Wagtails, on detecting the scent of Bob's hands on their babies, would discuss the matter excitedly for awhile, then either abandon, or fall upon them in a rage and kill them.

In this way Bob indirectly did a lot of harm, though less than was commonly wrought by "professional" naturalists. Like them he could plead that he was working in the interests of Science.

The Blue Wrens, who were honored with the title of Superb Warblers, were not so particular, or perhaps I should say that their parental instinct outweighed such prejudices. Though shy birds, the parents lingered about, exhibiting the greatest concern and anxiety, while Bob examined the babies in the palm of his hand. There were four in the brood, all so much alike in appearance that the sexes could not yet be determined. But he knew something about Wrens, and before placing them tenderly in the nest, he made a bet with himself that there was only one male among them.

He had no sooner turned away than the parents flew to the door of their home, and fussily inspected the premises and the inmates. The wide gapes and hungry cries of the latter proclaimed that all that was wrong with them was that they wanted more dinner. Though waited on by both parents, they had such ravenous appetites that they were always asking for more.

They were six days old when their eyes opened, and a week later they left the nest. Their tails were not more than an inch long at this time, and all wore a uniform greyish-brown plumage like the mother bird. This was an anxious time for the parents. What with feeding them, and teaching them to fly, and keeping them together, and instructing them to get under cover when menaced by an enemy, they were kept busy from morning till night. Then there was the trouble to get them to roost. The nest-bush was not now their home, but a low bushy tree near by. On a thin horizontal limb of this bush which stood a few feet from the ground, they would perch regularly till the following spring.

The mother would call and call as she led the way. She would flutter to the roost and back again, and, would keep them together when they wandered in different directions. She could not make them understand that they must roost now like

the Magpies across the gully, and the Magpie Larks in the box clump, instead of going back to the snug bed they had left. With a great amount of persuasion and no little patience, she at last got them on to the limb. When they were all perched side by side, she, thankful that her day's task was over, settled down at one end of the little row, with the male parent at the other end. In that position they camped every night.

Though the stone Curlews screamed wildly along the ridge, and the prowling dingo sent forth a lonely howl at intervals through the night; though the Teringing (Owlet Nightjar), and the Gooragang (Winking Owl) made weird noises by the river, and the Powerful Owl, who preyed on small birds, passed softly overhead, they feared nothing whilst thus snuggled between the little grey mother and the game midget in blue and black who was her life-mate. The bright, joyous days that followed had really more dangers for them, since the small fry were preyed upon by the common enemies much more than were the larger birds. The sweet-voiced Butcher Bird was a friendly neighbor to most of the feathered kind, but he had a craving now and again for a little poultry. At these times, he attacked any small birds that came his way, whether Wren, or Robin, or Finch. They were also easy game to the wild cats and the skulking fox, which waited for them in the undergrowth, and among the dense tussocks.

In such places, and in low detached covers that dotted the open grassy lands near scrubs, the Wrens, like the Robins and

Finches, loved to play, and sing, and feed. They were not gregarious like the Finches, which assembled in flocks of thousands, nor like the Tits and Chats and Robins, which, in a lesser degree, associated in colonies. The half-dozen kept always to themselves, and had their own bit of territory just as other individual families of Wrens had theirs. Each group of Magpies also had its own private hunting ground, and resented intrusion by other Magpies. Their territorial divisions, however, were of considerable extent, and embraced the numerous subdivisions claimed by the Wrens and other unrelated or distantly related groups.

Among the bushes, and through the grass, the parents led the infant quartette. They chatted and fed as they went. Though they could fly, they had yet much to learn. The most important lesson was how to find and catch their food, and how to prepare it for swallowing when they had caught it. The mother, having captured a caterpillar or a grasshopper, would welt it on the ground, run it through her beak, and crush it from end to end. She would then drop it, and try to induce one of the chicks to complete the process. After a moment, if unsuccessful, she would return to it, and chat encouragingly as though she were saying: "See, you take it up like this, hit it till it's limp, then nip it right along with your bill till it's soft. So!"

The manipulation finished, she would offer it to one of them with her beak, and hop nimbly away in search of something else. Moths, flies, including blowflies and March flies, beetles, larvae, cockroaches, and grubs were equally welcome, and with each find she uttered a soft note of satisfaction, and the lesson was repeated.

Such a simple lesson it looked yet they were many days learning it.

When they were a month old, their tails had grown to their full length, and they had so far mastered the art of providing for themselves as to be able to catch the nimble fly. Still, both

(Lawrence & Littlejohns.)
BLUEY, THE WREN (MALE).

(Lawrence & Littlejohns.)
THE BLUE WREN (FEMALE).

the adult birds continued to feed them for another six weeks. At times, they fed on the ground in the deep grass, where they met the Quail and her merry brood, and now and again were startled by encountering a foraging Brush Pheasant. The big bird meant them no harm, but his fierce-looking black head thrust through the tangle of blades, did not invite confidence. The Quail did not mind him in the least, except at nesting time, when she knew he would gobble up her eggs if he found them. The Wrens, however, always shifted quickly from his path. At other times they hunted and gambolled by turns in the low bushes. The cockbird displayed his handsome plumage, and now and again poured out a joyous summer song that drowned the squeaky notes of the youngsters.

The young ones were five months old before that budding naturalist, Bob Bucknell, noticed any difference in their appearance. Then the first moult took place. There was now a marked change in one bird. The others merely donned new coats of the same shade as the old. The solitary exception was distinguished by a light-blue tail.

"Didn't I say so!" Bob exclaimed joyously. "One bluey and three hens."

The blue color marked the male, and here Bob was up against a problem that had doubtless puzzled many a scientist. In most broods he had kept under observation, female birds predominated. Yet, in the breeding season, he had often noticed two, and occasionally three, males in attendance on one female, when all took part in feeding the young. At the same time there were always a number of unmated females. These, he concluded, were young birds. The females did not mate the first year, whilst the males did. In regard to the other matter, his father, who was an old bushman, explained that only one bird acted in the capacity of husband. The other was tolerated because he could not be driven away.

"But why doesn't he get a mate of his own?" Bob asked.

"He might be their own son, of the previous brood, who had refused to be turned out, or who has not grown enough to take up domestic duties on his own account. Or perhaps he hasn't been able to find a mate for himself. Small birds have so many enemies, and the females, who are less active and wary, suffer more than the males."

"They'd want to, to level things up," said Bob, "when there are so many more females hatched than males."

"There's another point," said his father. "Birds have their attachments like other things. Geese, for instance, are very affectionate. Most birds merely love for a season and then separate. Others, such as the Blue Wrens and Flock Pigeons, choose each a mate when a year or so old and stick to her for life, or until forcibly parted. Perhaps, in the time of choosing, two males are attracted by the same female, and the loser, who is too strongly taken up with her to go away and look for a substitute, becomes an outrageous nuisance and a disturber of the happy home. He haunts the premises and tries, maybe, to induce the little wife to elope."

"I suppose some of them do clear out with the other fellow?" queried Bob.

"In the case of a more masterful bird, that either happens, or he takes possession of her and the home, too."

Impressed by these remarks, Bob kept an untiring eye on his feathered friends. He always moved stealthily along by the river scrub, and kept under cover and picked his steps as he approached their haunt, for the Wrens flew off at any unusual sound. In this respect, they resembled the great Lyre Bird, to whom they were allied. First, he would hear the sharp note of alarm. Then one would fly off, and the others would follow in single file. They might hop actively about the bushes, chirping or singing the while, but they would not pursue their ordinary business whilst he remained in view.

BLUEY, THE WREN

Bluey, as he had named the male chick, was now the dominant member of the brood. He was very little bigger than his sisters, but he was stronger and smarter, and ever so much prouder. By virtue of these qualities, and the bit of blue he had acquired in his tail, he put them completely in the shade. He was a little more than ten months old when his second moult occurred. From this ordeal, he emerged the gayest little dandy that could be seen on a grass stem. Not only was his tail a darker blue, but his head was a beautiful blue also, and his bill was nearly black. He was now arrayed in full plumage, which was a lovely harmony of blues and blacks. His sisters eyed him with pride, and perhaps envy, for their own adult dress showed no change in color.

The Redbreasts, and the Flamebreasts and the Yellowbobs, who were friends of his, could flash fine colors, but no color was as showy as his. With his tail cocked straight up, he darted gaily from twig to twig, and practised the rollicking song of his kind, for it was high time for him now to take up his musical lessons in earnest. He was the showpiece among the feathered midgets in the light coverts by the scrub.

As before remarked, he was called the Superb Warbler, and when he had mastered the grand oratorio of his fathers, the title would be well-merited. Of the sixteen species of the genus "Malurus," some of whom were red-backed, some black-backed, and others marked with white on the back and wings, none could equal him in brilliance of song or dress. His smallest relative, whom he saw when he ventured down by the swamp, was the Emu Wren, who was a quaint little fellow with a light-blue throat and a tail which consisted of six shafts resembling emu feathers. The tail was four-and-a-half inches long, whilst the body measured only one and three-quarter inches. This tiny member belonged to a different group, which included the weird little Grass Bird, the Grass Wrens, and the Rock Warbler.

PART II.

The squeaky notes of his infancy began to leave him in July, and by August he had acquired his full song. How merrily he rolled it out, morn, noon, and eve. Often, too, in the early night, like Willy Wagtail and the Reed Warbler, he would rouse up suddenly and deliver himself of a brief but cheery song. If he missed his parents and sisters, when he hunted in the grass, he would at once bring the song to his assistance. Mounting a commanding twig, he would sing until he was answered, then fly off immediately towards the spot where he had heard the voice.

All this time, they had kept together, but no sooner had he become an accomplished singer than his father intimated to him that it was time for him to clear out. The first gentle hints were unheeded, and the old bird talked to him in anger, and pecked him whenever he came near. Bluey was surprised and dismayed. He could not understand this sudden change in his parent, who had been so long his ardent protector. In a humble spirit he went to his mother. That enraged her consort the more, and he attacked him fiercely and persistently until he had driven him off. A few days later the mother acted in the same way towards her daughters, and chased and beat them until they had all left her. So the family was disbanded, and almost immediately the old couple set about to prepare for their next brood.

Bluey, thrown on his own resources, was a lonely and miserable mite for the first couple of days. He moped among the bushes, and now and again chirped a dismal response to the merry voices about him. The dawning September with its wealth of scent and flower had stirred the Native Canary, who poured forth a delicious stream of melody. The Diamond Birds, Redcaps, and Tree Creepers were all more sprightly and busy, but he remained a sad little chap, and the persecution to which he was subjected did not tend to mend matters.

It was the season when his kind zealously guarded their respective patches, and attacked trespassing Wrens more determinedly than at any other period of the year. He had ventured up the river and down the river, and once he had crossed the stream, only to be driven back each time by the pugnacious males who had selected there. There did not seem to be any vacant land anywhere—except out back. As he was not of the wandering sort he found it hard to tear himself away from the old associations.

He was perching disconsolately in a distant part of his native towri (aboriginal name for the territory of a tribe) when the father bird, who was very fussily busy these days, caught sight of him. He did not ask him if he was married yet, nor did he bother to inquire why he was not elsewhere. He just lowered his head and rushed at him in silent fury. That determined him. Straight as he could go, he flew to a scrubby rise, far out from the river. On one side was a deep grassy gully, with here and there a clump of cockspur and other bushes on the high level. It was an ideal place for a Wren settlement. Communities of Robins, and a few Grass Warblers and Bush Larks, among others, helped to brighten it.

Whilst running and hopping down the slope in the mellowing hours, and now and again fluttering and darting, butterfly-like, over the red-topped grass, he met a lady of his own species whose greeting was very different from what he had been used to of late. In a little while he had forgotten home and mother. He proudly displayed his fine dress, and coquettishly turned and flicked his tail, whilst, with his whole heart in the effort, he sang his song of spring.

But he had to fight for his lady-love, for other young bluecoats who thought they had as much right to her as he had, had come to the hillside. The contest resolved into a desperate scrimmage between four. They were all fighting together to see who should have her. Hitherto, Bluey had soon turned tail when attacked by aggressive males, but then he knew that he was violating the laws of birdland. He was now fighting for his rights, for that which all warm bloods, whether bird or animal, will give stubborn battle.

From the conflict he emerged triumphant, and flew off ultimately in the happy possession of the maiden Wren. Their main concern was to select a patch sufficiently removed from other Wrens, and this they found at the head of the gully. Under a dense bush, three feet from the ground, the little hen built her nest, which was dome-shaped, with a side entrance composed of fine grasses and lined with feathers. The task occupied her six days, though, of course, she did not work at it all day long. Three small white eggs, marked with reddish-brown spots, were placed in the cosy receptacle.

All this while Bluey's demeanour proved that he was fully aware of his responsibilities. Active and pugnacious, he saw that no brother Wren trespassed on his selected run. The presence of the Cuckoos, who had just come down from North Queensland, he as hotly resented. Big as they were, he attacked them gamely and drove them away, and was often assisted in doing so by the Fantails, Flamebreasts, Tits, Wood Swallows, and Scrub Wrens. But they returned again and again, ever looking for other bird's nests, and, despite the vigilance of the Wrens, a Bronze Cuckoo succeeded in depositing her egg in the nest whilst they were feeding in the long grass.

They were not as wise as the Ground Tit, who covered the stranger's egg with grass so that it addled. Again, they were not as clever as the friendly Tomtit, who built a two-chambered nest, so that when the Cuckoo chose the top chamber, which was usually occupied by the male Tomtit, the egg remained unhatched. When the intruder placed her egg in the lower chamber before Mrs. Tomtit began to lay, the latter used the upper chamber, and the ends of the interloper were again defeated.

Mrs. Wren, though conscious of a change in her domestic arrangements, unfortunately, carried out the duties imposed upon her. The chicks appeared in fourteen days. Both parents fed them, at first with a joyous will, then with a growing mystified air. One bird was different, and ever so much bigger. He was a greedy giant whose capacious mouth was always foremost. He grew and grew till the domicile was crowded, and feeling uncomfortable, he shouldered the midgets out on to the ground. Gooloowee, the White Goshawk, who had been watching from a lofty perch for an easy meal, snapped up the first. Wolga, the Blue Falcon, made short work of another; and the third was carried off by Min Min, the Nankeen Kestrel, just as the frantic parents returned to the nest.

The stranger continued to grow. When he shortly left his cramped quarters to perch on a commanding branch, he was bigger than both his foster parents put together. Mrs. Wren was quite proud of her big baby. She danced and chirped with glee, and called to her mate to come and look at him. Bluey was astonished. He hopped round him excitedly, and surveyed him with a quizzical and suspicious eye.

"Good gracious," he seemed to say, "it must be an emu!"

The glutton kept them both busy in supplying him with food, and he further astonished Bluey by viciously attacking him for being slow with the dinner. The boy was master.

Bluey, who was simmering in an argument between his dignity

and his paternal instinct, felt that he ought to give the audacious youth a good pecking, if only on principle. He attended to his wants somewhat nervously. When the ungrateful youngster again pecked him, he promptly turned to correct him, and was as promptly thrashed by the infant.

Troubles came apace. He would not go to roost like other little birds, but chose his own camp, and Bluey and his mate humbly and timidly perched alongside him. His rightful owner, the Bronze Cuckoo, came early and late, calling, calling, while the big baby wailed dismally in reply. Rage and fear possessed the Wrens. Furiously, time after time, Bluey drove away the mother Cuckoo, but always she returned with the same appealing call, and ever that baby bird wailed in reply. Then came a day when he flew off with the Cuckoos, with the distracted Wrens flying wildly in pursuit, till the bigger, stronger birds were lost in the distance.

A sad little couple, they returned to the desolate home. Other Wrens were happy in their family circles. The Thrushes, Honeyeaters, Painted Quail, Blood Birds—all had their babies, but Bluey and his mate, with none, had no object in life.

Unlike most birds, whose families are disbanded early, the Wrens clung to their brood through all the year. So Bob was not surprised when presently they shook off their moping fit and set to work again to rear a second brood. This time their efforts were rewarded with three baby Wrens, with no stranger among them to repeat the tragedy of the spring. They were not the only late-comers of their species, for that terrible destroyer of birds, the imported fox, had been active in the neighborhood. Indeed many a pair, ruthlessly bereft of their first brood, had been forced to rear a second.

In the scented grass, and among the fruited bushes, Bluey attended them all day, and sang to them his grandest song. He fed them, and fought valiantly in their defence. If any danger threatened them, he rushed to the scene at the first squeak of alarm. He made no outcry. Not a chirp escaped him, but with lowered head and raised mantle, his wings and tail down, he charged swiftly and determinedly at whatsoever might be present. Birds, many times his size, he bluffed by his dash and courageous attitude. Having beaten or scared the enemy off, he would hop about with merry chirps as though crowing over the victory.

In the height of his glory, when summer was waning, what appeared to be a new calamity descended upon him. All his gay plumage fell away from him, and every vestige of his beautiful blues and blacks was lost. He sang no more, but cowed under the deep cover, and wondered miserably in his own way why this should be so.

As his new coat grew, he became more sprightly. The coat was a sober greyish-brown like his mate's and his children's. They did not seem to notice his lost grandeur, and he gradually became resigned to his altered state, though he was quieter and more retiring than formerly. Other male Wrens came on to his towri unheeded, and he went on to theirs without protest. All wore the same safe winter dress, and though maintaining their individual family circles, they could be said for the time to be sociable birds.

The Willy Wagtail, chirrupping good naturedly on a stump, or on the back of a browsing cow, cut a more dashing figure than any of them, during this period. But, in early spring, Bluey again moulted, when, to his great delight, his bright-colored plumage was resumed. Then he sang his best from the top of the bushes, and gambolled in the spring sunshine, as though he desired to show Willy Wagtail what an insignificant creature he was. Willy had only a black and white suit for all the year, whereas Bluey had demonstrated that he was a bird of fashion, who dressed suitably for the winter and summer seasons.

He might not sing as well as the Reed Warbler, or the Silver

Eye, but still his was one of the welcome voices of the bush. For the service he did in keeping insect pests in subjection, he was worth more than his weight in gold.

Each year a new nest was built, though the pair were always to be found about the same place. Many happy broods they reared before the partnership was ended. As he sat preening himself on an exposed twig one morning, the little Falcon swooped down suddenly, and, in a moment, the little brown mate was alone.

Kojurrie the Goanna

PART I.

It was a warm summer morning. From a low perch, the Kookaburra watched a clear spot near the bank of a grassy gully that wound along by a selector's house and into a scrub beyond. It was a loamy spot that bore indications of having been recently scratched over, and a movement of the soil had caught the bird's eye. It cracked and heaved, and out of it came a little black head, and two bright eyes blinked up at the interested bird. The latter made ready to pounce down for an appetising meal, for he recognized the newcomer as Young Kojurrie, the Goanna, who had just come out of his shell, which was buried a few inches underground.

Motherless, like the young Brush Turkey, and having similarly to depend on his own resources, and shape his own course from birth, he was fitted for the battle of life with a wonderful instinct that told him at once that the prying bird was no friend of his. He possessed enough inherent cunning to know in the first moments of his existence what to do in the emergency. He did not think of drawing back now that he had been seen, for the huge beak would dig into the ground and easily dislodge him. He took stock of his surroundings, noted the best cover at hand, and gently eased his shoulders and hind limbs in readiness for a dash.

He gradually drew himself out of the earth. First one front paw and then the other appeared, with the deliberation of a stalking Gecko. At that moment, the Kookaburra made a sudden swoop. As suddenly the watchful lizard sprang from the natural incubator, and, scurrying over the few feet of clear ground, plunged into a patch of thick grass where the tip of his tail just beat the bird's beak by an inch.

It was easy for him to conceal himself in grass or bushes, under bark and logs. Without wandering very far from his birthplace, he gathered sufficient food until he was eighteen inches in length. He kept mostly to the ground, and mounted logs and stumps. He sometimes climbed a little way up a low tree, like Kunni, the Jew Lizard, and Bungara, the Common Dragon, whom he frequently met while hunting for birds' eggs and small animals. He watched the Quails, Pipits and Ground Larks, and rifled their nests. He followed the tracks of the Pheasant and Black Duck, and when he found their treasures, he squashed each shell in his mouth and swallowed shell and all.

He watched the Crows, for their actions showed him where meat or a nest of eggs was to be found. From the ground he could not see very far. It would have taken him days to explore the whole locality unaided, whereas Crows, winging leisurely over the treetops, spied out everything in a few minutes. They were practically his scouts. Having been led by them to fresh killed meat, he drove them from it, and the indignant Crows had to wait until he had gorged himself and crawled lazily away. He did not take liberties with Mulyan, the Wedgetailed Eagle, nor with Moru the Whistling Eagle, nor even with the big Brown Hawk. They would not be bullied like the Crows.

The wind was another help to him, and guided him to carrion. By this means he discovered a dead cow some distance up the gully, where two other Goannas were banqueting. One of them was very old and bulky. He measured six-and-a-half feet from his nose to the tip of his tail, and was so fat that his long slim mate could lose him in a race up a tree or along the ground. He was fattening for his winter sleep, and would retire earlier than his active companions.

KOJURRIE, THE GOANNA

On the putrid meat Kojurrie fed day by day. Placing his hands against the carcase, he tore the flesh off with his teeth like a dog, but swallowed the pieces without chewing. He crawled between the bared ribs and through the hollow frame for tit-bits, and enjoyed an odor that was highly offensive to Kunni and Bungara, and to Bogi, the Blue-tongued Lizard. At night he slept in a hollow log near by, and emerged for his morning meal when the sun was warm and the grass was dry.

By the time winter arrived, he had accumulated two large flakes of fat—a store of food that would sustain him by absorption through the period of winter sleep. Now he sought a sunny spot, and burrowed deep into the ground. He filled up the passage as he went, and left but room for his body at the end. There, secure from all danger, and protected from cold and rain, he remained all the winter.

In the warming spring, when the land was green with grass and flecked with flowers, and the birds were singing and pairing and building their nests, he woke from his torpor and came forth again.

He was longer and slimmer, and very hungry. A flood had washed away the remains of the cow, but in a waterhole a little farther on was a bogged sheep. The cruel Ravens had pecked out its eyes. Feeding on the living meat was Dirrawong, his big sluggish companion of the previous season.

The aggressive look and attitude of the glutton warned him off, and turning aside he thrust out his long slender tongue in resentment. The tongue was forked and could be drawn back into a basal sheath. It was a distinctive feature, for the members of the small isolated group to which he belonged were the only lizards that possessed such a snake-like organ.

His head was long and pointed, and, like the body, covered with small scales. The eyes were protected with well-developed lids. The limbs were powerful, and the claws long and sharp.

His prevailing color was black. The neck and back were crossed with lines of small yellow spots. The under surface was greenish-yellow, crossed with black bands. The limbs were marked with broad yellow blotches, and the whip-like tail was covered with yellow rings, which were broader on the rear half.

Scientifically labelled Varanus varius, he was popularly known as Lace Lizard, Lace Monitor, and Goanna. By many people he was miscalled Iguana, a name that belonged to a group of Brazilian lizards, which were in no way related to the Varanids. There was no representative of the Iguanidæ in Australia.

Kojurrie followed the course of the gully in expectations of finding another sheep, or cow.

On the way he flushed a hen, which had been sitting on a clutch of eggs in long grass. He ravenously pounced upon them, and devoured egg after egg.

He had reached the seventh when a girl, who had been aroused by the cackling of the hen, surprised him at his feast. For a moment he hardly knew which way to run for a tree. He rushed off at a great pace for a few yards, then whipped round and scurried in another direction. The girl raced after him with a long stick which she held up in both hands.

He reached a tree just a yard in front of her, and swung smartly round to the back of it as the stick hit viciously at the root.

Ascending rapidly and spirally he kept out of view of the circling enemy until he was beyond reach. The girl doubled back. Kojurrie thrust out his tongue and corkscrewed the opposite way. When he had reached a height of about twenty-five feet, he stopped and looked down at her with a triumphant twinkle in his eye. The girl began to throw sticks. He watched their flight closely, and swung his head to left or right as they clattered near him. When one struck him on the butt of the tail, he showed his annoyance in his countenance. His tongue worked rapidly, and maliciously, as he climbed higher. Out of

KOJURRIE, THE GOANNA.

(O. Webb)

Goanna Climbing a Tree. *(A. H. Mattingley.)*

reach of the flying missiles, he flattened himself straight out along a horizontal branch.

From that vantage point Kojurrie watched the girl. A dog had now joined her. They went along the gully and in turn surprised Dirrawong. He raised his head, and his sulky looks disappeared. Dirrawong was so gorged that he had no chance of escape. The dog caught him by the back and shook him until he was dazed and crippled. Then the girl belabored him vigorously with her stick. She afterwards knocked the sheep on the head, and, dragging it to a heap of debris, set fire to it. On top of the pyre she threw the big goanna.

Kojurrie noted every little detail of that tragedy, and it remained in his memory for many a day. Still it did not prevent him from venturing to the fowl house. Attracted by the cackling of hens, he crept in. Clutching the edge of the first box with his hands, he lifted himself up and peered into the nest. It contained two eggs. He dropped half into the box, ate them both, and passed to the next nest. It contained a china nest-egg. He took it in his mouth and tried to break it. He dropped it and took it up again. He had never seen such a hard egg before. He took it on to the ground and tried his hardest, without any better result. It was a freak of an egg. He turned it round and round and wrestled with it several minutes. He only hurt his teeth, and at last he gave it up.

Finding no more, he crept round to the back of the kitchen. The door was open, and on the table were some savoury bones.

He entered with the manner of a burglar, and, after peering into every corner, and listening attentively, climbed on to the table.

Just then the girl entered, and in a moment slammed the door. His retreat was cut off, so he scuttled across the fireplace, and scrambled up the chimney.

Meanwhile the girl's cries brought her mother on the scene. Kojurrie saw them look up from inside as he balanced on the top edge of the chimney. The dog was yelping and dancing with excitement outside.

Before he could decide what to do next, he was roughly prodded from his perch with a clothes prop. Luckily he fell into the gutter between the sloping side of the chimney and the gable of the house. Then he climbed on to the roof, where he was kept a prisoner for hours.

Late in the afternoon the dog relaxed his watch, and Kojurrie stole down to the ground. For the first few yards he moved slowly, and looked from side to side. He then ran quicker and quicker, and, when well into the grass, made off at his fastest pace.

For the rest of that season he kept away from the house. He was an accomplished robber who could climb, run and swim with equal ease and skill. He chose his trees with good judgment, and peeped into every hollow knob and spout in search of eggs, young birds, and possums. Parrots' nests he robbed with ease, but the White Cockatoos, the Kingfishers and Magpies gave him such a buffeting that he generally kept away from their homes. His bedchamber was a hollow limb, and sometimes, when pursued and pelted with sticks and stones, he sought that refuge in the day.

He had some terrifying adventures. On the eve of winter, when he was growing sluggish, the selector chased him on horseback and flogged him to a tree with his stockwhip. The whip did little damage on his tough scaly body, but the resounding cracks made his heart jump with terror. As he climbed the gum bole the whizzing thong had more effect. It lapped round him no matter how quickly he tried to sidle away, and with a sound like a pistol shot.

Just when he thought he was safe, and had eased up to get his breath, he got on to a piece of partly-shedded bark, which came off suddenly, and down he dropped. He seemed a wildly whirling form that was mostly legs and tail.

The selector, who had followed him round, was on the point of riding away when the mishap occurred. Kojurrie dropped across the horse's loins, and catlike, stuck his sharp claws in and hung on. The startled horse bounded and snorted, and as the twenty claws again scratched and pricked him, and the hard tail whipped him across the flank, he lashed out and bucked with a vigor that threw the man spinning into the grass.

About the same time the Goanna dropped off unhurt, and whilst the frantic horse bolted across the paddock, he rushed off unseen through the long grass and scrambled breathlessly up another tree. Such was his excitement and confusion that, for a moment or two he hardly knew where he was.

Stretching himself along a lofty limb, he watched the scene with scintillating eyes, while the enraged man below walked around, and looked up trees. He did not shift from the spot till an hour after the selector had gone.

A rabbit, furtively moving from tussock to tussock, aroused him. He quietly descended, head downwards, and set after it. All the indignities he had recently suffered were forgotten. His whole attention was centred on capturing the unsuspecting Bunny.

He approached cautiously and silently. Every rod or so he stopped and raised his head slowly, but, like a cat, almost immediately lay flat again. When he was about ten feet off he paused, and, watching for a favorable opportunity, drew himself up for a supreme effort. Then he made a sudden rush, and, before Bunny could realize the cause of the disturbance, had seized him by the throat. Once fastened, neither teeth nor claws relaxed their grip until the victim's struggles had ceased.

Holding the body on the ground with his hands, the captor then tore it to pieces with his teeth. He left little but scraps of pelt and a part of the head.

Soon afterwards he retired underground for his winter sleep. All the Goannas disappeared from the bush. The Dragons, Kunni and Bungara, sought winter quarters in hollow logs. Bogi, the Blue-tongued Lizard, was snug under the root of a hollow tree.

PART II.

Kojurrie had doubled his length since the previous winter, and in the succeeding spring he was more vigorous, more aggressive and daring. For his kind there was always an abundance of food. A season that was bad for most other animals was a time of plenty for him, for almost any kind of meat, whether fresh or in the last stages of decay, was acceptable. He could reach it whether it was buried under ground, stuck in the top branches of a giant tree, or was floating far out in the water. He swam to a bogged beast or floating carcase without hesitation, ate his fill, and swam lazily back to land.

This spring, he had another interest beyond administering to his gluttonous appetite. It was quickly manifested on his meeting with a female of the species, who was accompanied by a presuming youth. He raised his head high, and stared haughtily and insultingly at the latter, who lifted himself similarly and poked out his tongue.

Kojurrie, hissing like a snake, advanced with deliberate step. The other turned slowly away, with head lowered, and directed malicious side glances at his rival.

Tamoi, the lady they both admired, was slim and sprightly, and in their eyes the fairest thing in the bush. To other creatures, the two sexes looked as like as two peas.

To his mate, the conquering male showed a gentleness and tenderness that belied his true nature. He was not as affectionate as Kunni, the Jew Lizard, who was a most loving and sociable creature for all his terrifying aspect when he raised his frill and opened his capacious yellow mouth, but he was constant. Having chosen his mate, he was united for life.

With a happy and important air he led her to dinner. He was drawn to the wedding feast by its far-reaching odor. The main item was a fat possum, which had been so long dead that all the fur had fallen off it. The repast was concluded with two small snakes and the entrails of a bird that a hawk had dropped.

They slept in the same tree at night. Sometimes, the night camp was a hollow log or a hole in the ground. A rabbit burrow was an acceptable bed-chamber, and also provided them with a fine banquet of young Bunnies.

At times they hunted in different trees, or were widely separated on the ground, though they were never apart very long. If Kojurrie happened, from a lofty point, to espy another Goanna prowling about in the vicinity of his mate, he got down without much loss of time, and ran across to see what the fellow's intentions were. He was not sociable. Tamoi was the only companion he desired. Though everywhere was common hunting ground, it was a law of the Goannas that each couple should keep separate. They each had their home spots, from which they never wandered a great distance in any direction.

A long waterhole in the grassy gully centralized the haunt of Kojurrie and Tamoi. Half-a-mile away on one side was a wide swamp, and on the opposite side lay an ironbark ridge, with a small lagoon at its foot.

The sloping ground near the lagoon had an attraction for

Tamoi. She haunted it for several days, roamed about in a searching, undecided manner, and rooted here and there to try the ground. At last she found a moist, sandy spot that suited her purpose, and there she scratched out a hole several inches deep. It was her nest, which was judiciously placed where the infant Goannas would have immediate cover, and where they need not seek far for food.

A dozen white eggs, with tough, flexible, skin-like shells, which measured two-and-a-half inches by one-and-a-half inches, were deposited in the hole and covered up to be hatched by the sun. When the laying was completed, the surface was carefully raked over so that the site could not be easily discovered. She kept an eye on the place, and occasionally scratched it over again, until the young ones were hatched. After that she gave them no further thought.

About that time Kojurrie came into conflict with Nurai, the Black Snake. He met many snakes in his wanderings. Some of them he hardly noticed, whilst at the mere sight of others he thrust out his tongue as he did at the man-beast. Nothing provoked him more than a surprise by Nurai. Equally repugnant to him were Marrakilla, the Brown Snake; Mugga, the Tiger Snake; and Tamby, the Death Adder. Deep, undying enmity existed between them and the Goannas.

Kojurrie stepped on to the black body of the snake in thick grass. With a low hiss, and with a fierce glitter in his staring lidless eyes, Nurai flattened his ugly black head in anger, and struck at him with lightning swiftness. Kojurrie whipped round and rushed at his enemy with open mouth. The snake dodged smartly, and again the quivering head, which arched for a moment a foot from the ground, darted at the Goanna, who screwed as quickly on to his side to protect his armpit. In the effort to bite and to avoid being bitten, their bodies became mixed in a dizzy whirl, and their tails, which whipped from side to side as they turned and twisted, thrashed the grass like a whirlwind.

Breaking away, they sparred a moment with swaying heads, and then charged each other open-mouthed. They again became a tangle of whirling bodies. The snake hissed and the Goanna uttered a snuffling, coughy sort of sound as they snapped and ducked, reared and swung, and rolled over and under.

On breaking away the second time, Kojurrie arched his back, and, with a sullen, disgusted look on his face, retired to the bank of the gully. He had been bitten twice, and with instinctive precaution, sought among the herbage the antidote that bushmen had long tried to discover, and that was known only to Goannas.

He chewed the herb until the green juice ran from the corners of his mouth. Then he returned and resumed hostilities with more savageness than before. The Snake had been bitten on the body, but Kojurrie's bite was not poisonous. He strove to sink his teeth into the neck, but as often as he snapped at it Nurai swung back or aside, and guarded against that deadly grip as skillfully as Kojurrie protected his throat and his armpits from the lethal fangs. Back and forth they swayed, and at intervals enveloped each other in a whirlwind of writhing coils and lashing tails. Breaking away and clashing again, with fierce hisses and snorts of fury, and spurred by an animosity that was æons old, they struggled in terrible earnestness for mastery.

Again and again the Goanna went to the gully, and each time returned to the combat with green and dripping mouth.

In the fourth bout he obtained a firm grip with his claws as he swung under, and in an instant his jaws closed on the Snake's neck. In vain the latter endeavored to envelop him in a crushing coil. Swiftly shifting from side to side, he eluded the violent contortions, and held on with his teeth till the Snake was killed.

After releasing his hold he fixed a still watchful eye on the slightly squirming body, and with arched back walked around it for some time before he quitted the place.

A thunderstorm had been brewing during the progress of the

fight, and, soon after he had joined his mate, it burst over them with terrific force. Blinded by the driving rain and pelted with hailstones, they crept into a hollow log, where they remained all night.

At sunrise the selector passed close by on his way down the paddock. Kojurrie had just come out, and before he had time to turn back, the man's dog rushed between him and his refuge. No tree being handy, the nonplussed Goanna ran to the only available upright, which was the selector, and in a twinkling scrambled up on to his shoulders. The unwilling host danced and roared, whilst the dog, yelping and barking, jumped round and round.

Under pain of the pricking claws, and fearful of being bitten, the selector bent gingerly down with the intention of lying prone, that his objectionable burden might take himself off.

Just as he dropped on to his knee the dog made a bound at the Goanna, and all three floundered in the grass. Kojurrie was first on to his feet, and quickly scuttled back into the hollow.

That adventure induced him to shift his headquarters to the ironbark ridge, and he did not visit the gully again till the following summer. In the succeeding spring he was four years old, and six feet long. During the next eighteen months he added another six inches to his length, and increased so considerably in girth, that he had little more than half his former speed and nimbleness in running and climbing. The dewlap under his throat became more pendulous as he aged and fattened. It was inflated when anything irritated him, and being of a yellowish-white color, the broadened surface made him conspicuous even on the rough bole of an ironbark tree. The dark color of the tree, harmonizing with his own dusky hue, had often served as a protection to him in his younger days.

Still, he saw many men and many dogs in the interval, but was himself unseen. As they approached, he sneaked slowly away to a big tree, and ascended on the opposite side. However, he did not always escape so easily. His hearing was not keen, and, when stalking his prey, or bent on some other important enterprise, he gave his whole attention to the object in view. In consequence of this action he was not infrequently taken by surprise. At such times he would lift his head with a jerk, then rush for the nearest big tree with the rustling clatter of a willy-willy whisking over dry leaves.

One autumn day, he was following the track of Tamoi across a sandy patch by the lagoon, when suddenly he saw the selector in front of him. In a couple of seconds he was scrambling wildly up a tree. Tamoi, watching unseen from another tree, saw the man, holding something in his hand that looked like a long club, follow him round the trunk. But it was not a club, for he pointed it at the climber, and from it came a streak of lightning and a clap of thunder. Kojurrie dropped instantly, and lay on his back at the feet of the terrible man foe.

And Tamoi knew, as well as the Crows and the Eagles, that Kojurrie would climb no more.

Karaway the Cockatoo

PART I.

MANY foolish little birds try to fly before they are strong enough, and so flutter to the ground, where they become easy prey to enemies. Karaway, the White Cockatoo, wasn't going to make similar mistakes. Barring accidents, he had a long life before him. Was not his great-great-grandmother over a hundred years old? There was, indeed, no need to hurry at the beginning. He was so well feathered, when his mother coaxed him out of the hollow spout at the top of a big red gum tree, that from the ground he and his parent looked as much exactly alike. From an ugly, clumsy-looking, almost naked, dark-skinned infant, who nodded and rocked his big head and squawked all day, he had become a sprightly and elegant bird.

He moved along the limb with claw and beak. The great distance to the ground made him afraid. The presence of hawks made him still more afraid. Several of them he knew well, for he had watched them secretly from the seclusion he had just left. From a top branch, directly above him, Gooloowee, the White Hawk, looked hungrily at him. From a neighboring tree Wolga, the Blue Falcon, eyed him with a fierce stare; whilst Bilbil, the

Sparrow Hawk, was perched beyond, and Jilli-jilli, the common Kite, soared overhead.

In looking up at the latter he almost lost his balance. In a panic he moved along the limb again with claw and beak, and cried to his mother. She still moved on, and, when she could get no farther, flew to another branch. Up he climbed, but he uttered all the while a monotonous, whining cry that had earned him more than one severe smack from his mother's hard bill in the nest. Then she flew to another tree. How he was to get there he didn't know. He raised his crest, stretched his neck, and fidgeted round and round and squawked. There was no branch or vine by which he could connect with her. Evidently he had to trust himself to the air the same as she did. After all, it looked easy; she just opened her wings, flapped them up and down, and away she went. Well—

Taking a tight grip of the limb with his strong claws, he spread his wings and exercised them vigorously. Harder and harder he strove till he almost tore his claws from the wood. In this way he tested their strength and lifting power. A dozen times he was on the point of making the plunge, and each time he barely mustered sufficient courage to let go with his feet. When he finally did so, he flew quite strongly, and alighted successfully in the other tree, where he proudly erected his yellow crest and joyously cackled, as much as to say, "Did you see that?"

Karaway was twenty inches in length, plump and well shapped, and the whitest and the largest of the white cockatoos. His elongated, recurved, occipital crest was a beautiful deep yellow, and he was sometimes called the Sulphur-crested Cockatoo. In addition to this conspicuous helmet, his general snow-white plumage was relieved with pale yellow round his ears, in the centre of the under surface of the wings, and on the basal portion of the inner webs of the tail feathers. His bill was black, powerful, and abruptly curved. His eyes were black; his feet were greyish-brown.

By degrees, he made his way to the side of a quiet lagoon, where, in low, bushy trees, a small company of his kind were camping during the midday hours. They were silent, but not inactive, for they had a mischievous habit, at such times, of snipping leaves and branchlets off the trees, especially off the wild apple, just to test their bills.

Karaway was no sooner amongst them than he was engaged in the same mischief. It was just what he had been wanting for the purpose of exercising his strong bill. The inclination to bite and saw was irresistible—a habit peculiar to almost the whole of the parrot tribe. In numerous places throughout the vast forest, his associates betrayed their camps by the leaves and bark they stripped off, and the scars they left on the branches. Still, though they were immensely superior in numbers, the damage they did was comparatively insignificant to that done by the black cockatoos.

These dusky relatives, numbering seven species in all, moved in small parties. They fed on eucalyptus seeds, banksia, wood grubs and caterpillars, and, despite their severe pruning of forest trees, did a lot of good in keeping in subjection certain pests.

HEAD OF COCKATOO, SHOWING POWERFUL BILL.

Their flight was heavy, and most had a low, crying call. They laid two white eggs, which were placed deep down in lofty spouts. Two notable features were the marking of the tail and the depth of the bill. The black tail of each had a broad stripe down all but the two central feathers. The stripes of the Banksian were deep vermilion; of Leach's Cockatoo, scarlet; Wyla, the Funeral Cockatoo, freckled brimstone yellow; White-tail, or Baudin's Cockatoo, creamy white. Larawuk, the Great-billed Cockatoo, had the most powerful bill, which was one-and-a-half inches long and three inches deep. He also had the longest crest. The bill of the Karrak, or Western Black Cockatoo, was two-and-three-quarter inches deep; the tail was marked red. The Yellow-eared Cockatoo, who was twenty-four inches in length, and had a light buff-colored band, thickly mottled with grey, was the most showy of the black family. In common with some of his dusky cousins, he flew low on the approach of rain, and uttered a whining cry. To get the grubs in gum and wattle trees he scooped off the bark and cut thick branches right through. So powerful was his bill that he cut down saplings six inches thick, and tore out pieces ten inches long. The Great Palm Cockatoo, who had a large, bushy, black crest, and crimson and yellow on the cheeks, was the only one whose tail was all black. He fed on the tender shoots of palms in northern scrubs.

Besides these seven "black Australians," and six white or rose-tinted, he had one grey relative—the Gang Gang. They made a total of fifteen varieties. Though the Corellas, Galahs and Weejuglas mingled together on the inland plains, the large white birds of the sulphur crest kept always to themselves.

From their midday camp they flew down on to a small plain in twos and threes till only Karaway remained. The journey to the lagoon had fatigued him; he was not going to travel any farther yet, if he could help it. He could see them easily. They were all close together and busily moving about on the ground. Perhaps they would come back soon.

His soliloquy ended in a startled screech.

Holding with one foot, he scratched his poll with the other and talked to himself. In the midst of this pleasant occupation, Moru, the Whistling Eagle, alighted on a limb within three feet of him, and his soliloquy ended in a startled screech. With his head thrown excitedly forward, and his crest raised, he edged away with quick side steps, but kept an alert eye on the enemy. When the Eagle advanced, he half opened his wings and his mouth at the same time, and hissed. Still the Eagle advanced. Alternately hissing and ejaculating, he turned nervously from side to side. When the Eagle made a more determined advance, he jerked his head violently towards him, and uttered a sharp, clicking note. Moru halted for a moment, but he was not scared. He came on again. Karaway, unable to back any farther, made a wild dart for a higher branch. After a brief interval the Eagle flew to one still higher. The cockatoo immediately realized the advantage of the position, and, throwing himself into the air, winged desperately towards his companions.

Before he had gone fifty yards the Eagle swooped at him. He dipped almost to the ground, and, in attempting the abrupt turn that would take him sharply aside and upward, he tumbled on to his back in the grass. His frantic gesticulations and loud screams brought the company flocking over him before the Eagle could get round for another swoop.

They gathered him in their midst, and their excited cries drowned his complainings. When they settled again on the plain, he was too upset to feed. He appointed himself sentinel for the flock, and kept a sharp look-out for hawks, whilst the rest regaled themselves on seeds, roots and bulbs.

Towards sundown they mounted high, and, calling loudly to one another, flew some miles away to a retired roosting place on a gentle rise.

They were astir again at dawn. After a repast of eucalypti seeds, roots, and a fungus known as Blackman's bread, they went still farther afield. Of vagrant habits, they travelled hundreds of miles, making temporary homes wherever food abounded. Their kind encircled the continent, extending for a considerable distance inland, though they never ventured into the dry central parts of the country; and, unlike the Magpies and other birds that preserved exclusive colonies, and whose movements were restricted within certain territorial limits, they joined forces with mutual satisfaction with all flocks of their own sort wherever they met them. They frequented the open plains, the cleared lands, and the thinly-timbered, gently undulating country, in preference to the densely-timbered regions favored by the black cockatoos.

Almost daily they gathered at a waterside to drink and bathe—sometimes after the morning meal, sometimes in the afternoon. They always had their quiet midday camp in open forest country by a river or lagoon; and ever, in all seasons, they kept their snow-white coats spotlessly clean. The young Cockatoo, after he had washed and preened himself, put on more airs than the gaudiest parrot that sported amidst gum blossoms. For a couple of weeks his mother assisted in providing him with food; then she cast off all responsibility. He was one of the immense flock, one of a vast socialistic community whose numbers were unlimited.

PART II.

At the end of autumn they flocked from all parts to the agricultural areas, and formed an enormous concourse that met in noisy council on the slope of a clear hill. Upon a hundred trees they clustered so thickly that the trees looked snow-covered. For five minutes Karaway was struck dumb with astonishment. His black eyes scintillated with excitement as he viewed the great assemblage; his crest rose and spread as his roving glance went from tree to tree. When he at last gave voice to his feelings, he could not hear himself cackle for the noise; he could hardly hear himself scream!

On a lofty branch in their midst perched General Ny (Nyeuk-an), looking very wise, and endeavoring to sift some meaning from the uproarious debate. Ten thousand birds spoke at once, with scarcely a lull. Some more boisterous than others flew noisily about; a few peevish ones fought and screeched when they were crowded by their associates.

After an hour or so, the excitement and clamor died down, and the council got to business in more orderly fashion. It was the time when the corn was beginning to ripen on the farms; when every farmer watched for the cockatoos with a loaded gun. Every year they had raided the crops, and pitted their cunning against the grower. Hundreds of their compatriots had been killed; hundreds more had been wounded. There were still a few among them who had only one leg; several had only one eye. Still, they must have a feast of the delicious grain.

Karaway, the Cockatoo

MATES.

Over a vast extent of country, which embraced hundreds of square miles, there might be, at this season, only a small patch here and there ripe enough for their purpose. Their object was to discover those patches and make a concerted raid upon them.

Long after midday the council discussed the matter. By that time many of the councillors had gone to sleep; others, with closed eyes, nodded and rocked lazily on their perches. General Ny, observing that there was not a wakeful quorum, roused them to sudden attention with a piercing screech. Then he gave orders to his captains—the old cock birds who had been leaders of little companies that had been distributed about the country during the lean months. These shortly flew away, and each, followed by fifty to a hundred of the rank and file, flew off in a different direction.

With the contingent that flew due west was Karaway. He was excited and felt quite important, but hardly knew yet what it all meant. They numbered about eighty birds. Ten miles from the starting point, at a signal from the captain, a dozen detached themselves and went off to the left. Shortly afterwards another detachment went off to the right.

Each of these detachments had a leader, who called out on leaving the main body, and continued to call at short intervals until he had got well away with his complement. His calls were responded to by members of his band; thereafter, excepting for a brief colloquy now and again, they were silent.

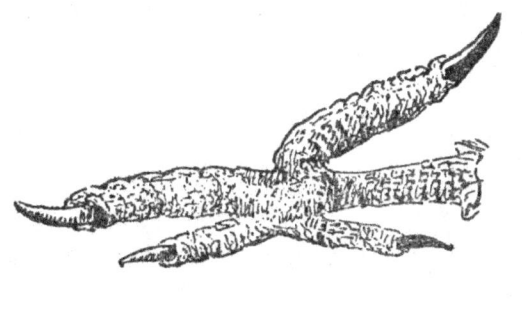

FEET OF A COCKATOO.

Detachments continued to break away until only a dozen were left. These alighted in a tree forty miles west of the main camp. After a rest, they commenced to feed for a while in the trees, then on the ground. At dusk they roosted in the vicinity.

With the dawn they went off in several small lots on various courses. Karaway's lot, still going west, numbered three. They travelled leisurely, and fed wherever any food offered, until they came to a river farm where the corn leaves were turning sere. They settled in a high dead tree on the bank, where they remained very quiet for half-an-hour. Then one flew down to the corn, and was followed shortly by another. Karaway had been deputed sentinel; it was his duty to remain in the tree and keep watch. He was hungry himself, and his mouth watered for a few grains of corn, but, with commendable faithfulness, he watched unselfishly whilst his comrades were feasting below.

He saw farmer Slocum come out, stand at the back of the house, and look towards him. There was perfect safety in the distance between them, so he did not say anything about it.

With Mr. Slocum was a hired boy whose unpleasant duty through the cold months was to "mind Cockatoos."

"Cockatoos," Mr. Slocum instructed him, "can talk to one another just the same as you and I can. Every year I've noticed two or three come to the farm when it was about time for the corn to mature. Perhaps mine would be a little backward, and, after sampling it, they'd go away, flying higher, and I'd hear no more of them for a time. But, if the corn's ripe enough, as it is now, I can assure you it's a good day's work to shoot the scouts; otherwise, in a few hours, you'll see cockatoos swooping down on to the crop from all sides. Sometimes they come in the dusk, all silent as Quakers, and roost in neighboring trees; then they drop down quietly in the grey dawn, have a good breakfast, and go away boasting about it. When you get up in the morning and see one cocky sitting very quiet in the tree-top, you can be sure there's a banquet going on below him. They never utter a word while they're feeding, for they're all stripping hammer and tongs, and listening for the watchbird's 'look-out.'"

The sentinel kept an alert eye on them as they came down the cart-track through the corn. When they were within a quarter-of-a-mile, he uttered a sharp, clicking note. Instantaneously, his two compatriots flew up. On the dead limbs, beside him, they wiped their bills and discussed the approaching foe. The leader of the trio was an old bird, who knew well that the thing the man carried under his arm was a gun—a dreadful thing that roared like thunder and flashed like lightning. He had a scar on his leg where a shot had struck him years before. He uttered a warning cry, and they flew across the river.

"Now," said Slocum, "we must try and trick them. They'll watch us away; so we'll pretend to go home, then double back through the brush along the bank, and wait for them. We must move very quietly, and keep under cover all the time."

For an hour the three thieves waited. Then, one by one, they returned to the tree over the corn. There they lingered another half-hour before they renewed the attack on the crop. This time the old bird was sentinel.

Karaway, who was hungry, was the first to dive down. Clinging to the side of a corn-cob, he stripped the husk down from the top with his bill, and, one by one, shelled the grains right round. From each grain he scooped the kernel with his under mandible, and held the remainder in his foot while he bit it up into small pieces.

He had not been feasting very long before the sudden shock of a gun nearly shook him from the cob. As he rose, he saw the sentinel drop. Loose feathers floated slowly downward from the tree. A second shot immediately afterwards cut short the flight of his mate. With frantic cries, he flew across the river and perched alone in a distant tree.

Breathlessly gasping, and with his heart in a flutter, he waited and watched and listened. Slowly he realized that his mates were lost. He did not like being alone at any time; under such tragic circumstances he was painfully nervous. At last he rose very high in the air, and made a bee-line for headquarters.

Other scouts joined him on the way, and they returned to camp, where they boasted loudly of the daring deeds they had performed, and of the lands of plenty they had discovered. The day closed to a deafening clamor of voices, for each band of scouts seemingly endeavored to talk down the others. Nevertheless, the reports were intelligently interpreted, for next day the whole flock departed in several large divisions, and each division went direct to a field of ripe corn. Slocum's farm was not visited; for more than a week that quarter was shunned by the whole community.

At most farms they met with a warm reception, and their casualties were heavy. But the grain was sweet, and they were no sooner driven from one field than they descended boldly upon another. Only when they met with immediate and determined resistance on all neighboring places did they abandon their siege and go away to a distant section. Eventually they came to levy from Slocum's crop. Karaway led them to the locality. They set out with tumultuous cries, but, long ere they came near the farm, dead silence reigned among them. Like sheeted ghosts they arrived in the dusk, and whitened the trees along the river.

When day dawned, only one innocent-looking bird was visible among the trees. But what a sight he looked down upon! Ten thousand silent birds were enjoying a glorious breakfast, and were husking, shelling, and eating with the greatest rapidity. They made little noise in the process, for there was hardly any fluttering. Each one kept to the cob he had settled on. Here and there two birds clung to the same one. Occasionally a dry stalk broke under the weight, and there was a momentary disturbance. Otherwise their conduct was the most complete exibition of silence that could be found among birds who were so very noisy when noise did not matter.

Shortly, the sentinel observed the boy running down. At his signal, they rose like a great white cloud. A shot at long range hurried them to perches beyond sight of the farm.

They made a great uproar as they departed, but, hours later, they returned without a sound. The boy was working at a corner of the field, and, when he rushed towards them, they saw he had no gun. He shouted and coo-eed, clapped his hands and waved his hat; they answered with derisive cackles, and merely flew from one spot to another. When he had pursued them to one end of the farm, they flew back to the other, and were busily stripping long before he could get up to them.

Tired of running and shouting, the boy resorted to strategy. Picking up a stick, as near the shape of a gun as he could get, he held it in his hands in the manner of a stalking gunner, and approached as though he were trying to get a shot at them. They saw him steal into the corn, where they got sight of him only here and there. Each time he came nearer to them, and they became alarmed. In a body, they darted from the trees, and their rising flight as they passed over the forest showed that they were going right away for that day at least.

They continued to come on other days, until the last cob had been cut and stored in the barn. At the end of the harvesting, they flocked on to the farms for the gleaning. Cobs that had been missed, loose grain on the ground, and other pickings that such fields provided, kept them well supplied for a couple of weeks. They were not now secret in their comings and feastings; their many chattering voices could be heard for miles. Nor did they bother much about keeping a watch. When they reposed by some quiet lagoon, they often remained unconcernedly in the trees, though the farmer, looking for ducks, passed under them with his gun. After harvest there was peace between the farmers and the cockatoos.

The winter had been a strenuous and exciting time. In August, they sorted themselves into pairs for the more sober duties of domesticity. The couples formed into companies, which varied in numbers according to the facilities for nesting in the chosen localities. Ever sociable, unselfish, and exceedingly gregarious, they claimed no special rights over such localities. Indeed, the exigencies of the season alone confined each division to a certain area.

Karaway, who, like most long-lived birds, had been slow in coming to maturity, dallied long ere his fancy turned to thoughts of love. Many of his age, unchanged by the quickening spring and the ripening summer, and ready to brave again the guns of the angry farmer, were fated never to marry.

Finding a lady who took his fancy, during the restful, idle hours in shady trees, he went up to her in a half-cheeky, half-hesitating manner and kissed her. The lady raised her crest as if she was surprised, if not offended, at his impertinence. Karaway bowed humbly, and made some remarks about the weather as he twisted and fidgeted beside her. She turned her head away, and pretended to be absorbed in the doings of some cockatoos on a higher branch. He pinched her gently on the wing, at which she smacked him smartly with that member, and gave vent to a raucous screech.

The rebuff caused him to stand off until, calming her ruffled feelings, she scratched the back of her head with her foot. Then he edged up again, and, gently putting in his beak, considerately scratched the part for her. Slowly she put down her foot. At the same time, she held her head down to assist his efforts, while her dark eyes twinkled with pleasure. He also nibbled lightly at her shoulder, and stroked her beak with his own. Her maidenly reserve disappeared; she was captivated by his devoted attention. Looking very happy, they presently flew off on their honeymoon.

They would rejoin the company in leisure moments, but,

for a time, they were much by themselves. They had to find a suitable place for a nest. In the course of this search, they visited many trees, wound their way into many hollow spouts, and had long discussions and arguments about the holes they inspected. Old General Ny, whose experiences in house-hunting covered a period of more than three-quarters of a century, remembered when houses could be got almost anywhere. And Cockatoos were far more numerous then than they were now. Man destroyed the trees wherever he went, and the task of finding a fitting domicile became greater every year.

The search was not lacking in adventure. Many holes contained possums, who were indignant at the birds' intrusion into their bedrooms. In one was the burglar Kojurrie looking for eggs. He gave Curry, the bride, such a fright that she would not afterwards enter a hollow unless she could see to the bottom. It had to be a very lofty spout. The Parrots nested at any height, even close to the ground, and they betrayed their domiciles by biting the bark and wood away around their doors. But Curry was a wise, calculating bird.

Eventually, they selected one at the top of a giant gum tree. Some improvements were needed to make it habitable, as jagged pieces of dead wood stuck out from the sides. With their powerful bills, these were soon cut away and ejected. During their carpentering, they were careful not to make any mark at the entrance that could be seen from the outside.

On the dry wood dust at the bottom she laid two pearly-white eggs. Each one was a little more than an inch-and-a-half long by an inch-and-a-quarter broad. She never approached or departed from that nest in sight of an enemy. She came and went swiftly and silently. Her observation tree, from whence she darted to the nest, and on which she alighted after leaving it, was half-a-mile away. Thereabouts Karaway perched, when he was not with his male friends, while his partner was sitting. It was not discreet to linger about the nesting tree, as that would draw attention to it. So it happened that the male members of the local flock were much together, often miles away, while their consorts were hidden in the hollow spouts that led to their nests.

When the infants were hatched, he had less time to spend with his friends. Still, the members mingled together whilst searching for food. The husbands vied with their wives in boasting of the merits of their young ones. They were voracious infants, and called for food all day. They had to be fed by the parents for two months. Whilst Karaway waited on one, Curry attended to the wants of the other.

Large flocks were roaming over their areas, long before these belated youngsters were feathered. As soon as they got them on the wing, they joined the gay throng. Many of those who had mated early had nothing to show for their labors, for, in November, the bird-snatchers had been busy where the nests were accessible.

With the ripening of the crops, the multitude of pilferers returned to the farms. Day after day, the clamor of the hunted brigades resounded along the river. In a deep bend, after their first raid, they saw dead Cockatoos stuck on gibbets in exposed positions above the corn. From a safe distance, they examined the disquieting objects, and, after an excited consultation, departed in haste for the next plantation.

Karaway, with a thousand comrades, settled quietly in a tree that overlooked a promising field. A small flock of King Parrots feasting on the edge near the brush suggested safety, so down they dived.

Before they had time to strip their cobs the sentinel's sharp note of alarm called them back again. As they rose in a mass over the gully, half-a-dozen blackfellows sprang from cover on each side, and sent a dozen boomerangs that whizzed amongst them. These deadly weapons broke necks, legs and wings. Karaway and a score of his mates tumbled screeching to earth.

He realized, as soon as he hit the ground, that his only chance of escape now was to hide, and he made a desperate effort to scramble through the thick growth. But the trailing wing handicapped him. A black man tore through the bushes and vines and attacked him.

Screeching frantically, he fought with the ferocity of a wild cat, and, getting hold of a finger, he almost severed it from the hand with his sharp beak. Unable to use a club in the thicket, his captor grasped him savagely by the neck, and held him tightly until his life ebbed out.

BOORABY THE KOALA.

PART I.

THOUGH the first days of the young Koala's existence were passed in very much the same manner as those of the young Possum, he was not carried in the pouch until he was able to take care of himself. He was only a little fellow, and no bigger than an active kitten. He was, however, well covered with light grey fur when his mother hoisted him on to the back of her shoulders, and gave him to understand that he had to stop there and hold tight. She, of course, could not climb and reach for gum leaves and hold him at the same time.

At first he thought "piggy back" was fine fun. When she crept out of the big hollow knob that was her home, and walked along a slender limb a hundred feet from the ground, he dug his sharp nails in with fear.

It was a cold starlit night. Possums were feeding in the same tree, and Squirrels darted through the air a little way off with peculiar cries. He glanced timidly at them from time to time, but he was so much taken up with the danger of his position, that he could give little attention to anything else. The mother moved with slow, deliberate steps; nevertheless every movement made him fancy he was going to fall. Learning to ride in such a situation seemed a foolhardy undertaking. Indeed, it was absolutely dangerous.

Certainly, the mother ran no risk of falling; the great grasping power of her claws precluded that. Numbers of her kind, when they had been wantonly shot by settlers, had cheated their slayers by hanging under the limb in death as a Sloth hangs in life.

Perching herself in a small fork, the mother Koala grasped a branchlet in her hand, and, for some minutes, munched the juicy leaves. Then she retraced her steps, and started down the perpendicular trunk of the tree for the ground. It was a fortunate circumstance that she descended backwards. In this respect, the Koala differed from the Possums, Dasyures, and other Australian tree animals—with the exception of the Boongarry, or Tree Kangaroo. Still, Booraby, the youngster, was mightily uncomfortable. Clinging tightly to the dense fur of his mother, and looking anxiously from side to side as she dropped lower and lower, he scarcely breathed until the long, slow descent was accomplished.

On the ground, he could ride with ease and confidence. Like a little boy who has got over his first fears on the back of a pony, he even wanted to "show off." While she dug for succulent roots, he partly sat up and scratched his ear and his ribs. He had more leisure to admire the scenery, and to notice what was going on about him.

Madam Koala moved along the edge of a narrow belt of scrub that lined the river bank. It was, to him, a pleasure excursion, full of interest, for there were many other creatures abroad. The frisky Possums, with their gambollings and chasings, their squeaks and purring chatter; the Squirrels, with their sudden flights and squeals; and the night birds calling overhead, enlivened the passing hours. Boo, the Bandicoot, was busily rooting about in the grass. Murura, the Red-necked Wallaby, was clipping the tender herbage. Just inside a fence which they came to after a couple of hours' ramble, Parrimalla, the Scrub Wallaby, was enjoyably nipping down a patch of young corn.

She did not go through the fence, but turned out into the forest. She knew the thieves would be hunted with guns and dogs, for she had seen it happen many a time while she had been squatting quietly in an adjacent tree. She knew the farmer was also unfriendly to her, though there was nothing he could say against her. She never stole anything, and she never harmed anybody. Quiet and inoffensive, she asked for nothing but wild roots and the leaves of her native trees. Besides, she was one of the most attractive features in the bush. But there was no accounting for the actions of man. He turned his murderous hand equally against Kogra, the Echidna, and Duckbill, the Platypus, although they were not only as inoffensive as herself, but did good service for him in their unobtrusive ways. It had been a good world to live in before man had come, but now the struggle for existence was bitterly hard. Even when he did not directly molest her kind, he drove them before him by destroying every tree that nature had provided for their subsistence.

A deep snort overhead suddenly disturbed her meditations. Looking up, Booraby espied father Koala sitting in a small box tree. He had not seen much of his father, for that worthy was not very fond of society. He was often promenading about in the daytime, or drowsily sitting in some forked branch where daylight happened to find him. Nevertheless, Mrs. Koala, with some idea of asserting her rights, climbed up to him. Beyond a stertorous growl by way of greeting, and a solemn survey of the youngster, he took no notice of them. Externally the couple were alike. Mr. Koala, however, had a couple of white patches on the hind part of his back. Mrs. Koala had not these patches, and, whereas her broad ears were well marked with white, his were margined at the ends with black. But such marks were mere color variations. One or two of their neighbors, whose donkey-like cries they heard from time to time, were more than half white, whilst others were all grey.

Mrs. Koala brushed her little burden against her mate as she seated herself in a convenient position. Her look and manner were inviting.

"I think you ought to hold the baby while I get my supper."

Pa Koala looked at the baby with eyes that plainly said: "Let the little one get down and walk."

She caught the branchlet he was holding and pulled it rudely away. Pa Koala was decidedly vexed. He looked at her a moment as though he had a mind to knock her off the limb. However, he thought better of it, and shifted to another branchlet.

Being a long way from home, and a slow traveller, she left early, whilst he remained in the box tree, quite indifferent to the flight of time. As day was breaking, she climbed back into her nest. Booraby was glad to be home again. He was tired from so much unaccustomed riding, and a little bit stiff from clinging to a perpendicular back whilst he was being carried up and down trees. He rolled off with a sigh of relief, and, after a drink, coiled himself up in his mother's arms and went to sleep.

He had no fears when he went out again. He was quite at home on his mother's back, and enjoyed being carried about among the branches. As he grew older, he plucked some of the leaves within his reach while she was feeding, and, sitting up like a little jockey, munched them with enjoyment. When he was on the ground, he would slip off sometimes and beg for some of the roots she was digging up. He gradually got into the way of scratching for himself. Again, he would dismount on a limb, and either amuse himself by climbing about, or sit beside her and eat off the branchlet she held in her hand.

His next step was climbing a little way up the trunks and backing down again. Occasionally, she climbed a sapling without him, and when he was able to follow her successfully she showed a disinclination to carry him any further. When he seemed tired, or the climb was a stiff one, and he cried and whimpered like a child, she would, as a favor, put him on her back. But by-and-bye he cried in vain. There was no more "piggy-back" for Booraby; he had grown too large and heavy for those baby habits, and must now walk.

One morning, when he would have followed her into the hollow as usual, he was refused admittance. The bedroom was too small for both, and, as he was more restless and less regular in his hours of repose than the female sex, she complained that, with his fidgeting and scratching, she could not get her proper day's rest.

Day found him sitting disconsolately on the doorstep. He was dozing off when some Kingfishers and Magpie Larks discovered him. They made sport of him, and flew at him and pecked him. Indeed, they made such a disturbance, that no nocturnal creature in the neighborhood could get a wink of sleep. Booraby, ordinarily of a gentle disposition, was stirred into a fit of passion by their persecution. He warded the attacks with his hands as well as he could, and made a vengeful grab now and again as an incautious tormentor flew closely in front of him. His strong teeth snapped hard together like a steel trap when one darted just over his nose. He was forced at last to seek shelter. Over the roof of his old domicile was a thick cluster of foliage, and under that he hid himself.

The seat was as smooth as glass, and showed that another form had been wont to rest there. It suited him very well through the remainder of the warm weather. About the end of autumn, his father claimed it, and he was compelled again to seek fresh lodgings. Thereafter, he did not care much where he slept. Usually, if day did not surprise him in an uncongenial neighborhood, he sought a comfortable fork very high up from the ground. Though in the open, he was not easily discovered as long as he sat tight and remained quiet. He was wise enough to do this if there was an enemy in sight, for his color harmonized well with the grey and white of the gum trees. Unlike the Possum, the Flying Squirrel, and other arboreal animals that were most active at night, he rarely sought the seclusion of a hollow by day. Essentially an open-air creature, he found that almost any place at all suited him for a bedchamber.

Wet, windy days in such exposed positions were unpleasant.

Booraby, the Koala.

HE WAS QUITE AT HOME ON HIS MOTHER'S BACK.

However, the cold did not affect him, for he was encased in a thick, tough skin which was covered with soft fur that was fairly long and dense. His ears were of moderate size, but as they were covered thickly with hairs two inches long, they looked large and rounded. His nose was black and prominent; his hands and feet were large and white. The hands were composed of two sets of fingers; the two innermost were opposed to the three outer, and all were armed with big, curved claws. The toes, excepting the innermost, were similarly armed. The exception was nailless, and placed in the same position and used in the same manner as the human thumb.

Though admirably fitted for climbing, he was tardy in his movements. He made certain of each hold as he went along; slow but sure. From this fact, some of the first white men who saw him named him Native Sloth. He was afterwards generally called Native Bear.

PART II.

His species associated in pairs, though many of them were much of their time alone. He had no yearning for their society. Nor did he show any enthusiasm when Yarri, an old acquaintance, came on to his branch as he rose from his solitary meal in a big blue gum. He resented the intrusion. But the visitor took no notice. He was a droll warrior who was not easily turned from anything he had set his mind upon, and he had set his mind on a bunch of choice young leaves that overhung a comfortable seat.

They came together with mutual growls. There was no room to get past. The intruder, who was the bigger of the two, edged an inch or two farther. The movement brought forth another growl from Booraby, and he struck at him with his claws. Yarri at once reared up, and, grasping the other with both hands, endeavored to throw him off. Booraby, holding to the limb with his powerful toes, fought fiercely with tooth and claw. For a moment or two, they rocked and swayed, and made a noise that could be heard a mile away. Suddenly, they both toppled over, and the combat ended with a thumping fall to the ground.

With a parting snort or two, and eyes that blinked savagely, Yarri climbed slowly back into the tree, whilst Booraby walked off in search of other pickings.

That morning, he did not seek a perch, but sat drowsily at the foot of a large tree. There, a prowling Dingo came upon him unawares. He sat up and looked at the disturber of his slumbers with an air of mild protest, but with no suggestion of alarm in his attitude or expression. The Dingo had too much respect for his ready claws to approach within reach of them. He moved from side to side, and waited a chance to get a snap at him from behind. Now and again, he looked round as if expecting assistance. Instead of that, a boy came along the bridle track that led past the tree, and at the sight of him the Dingo turned tail and fled.

Booraby regarded the newcomer with equal indifference. The boy prodded him with a stick, and provoked a murderous look and a grunt from him. Striking a defensive attitude, he tried to parry the prods with his hands until the boy poked him on to his feet. When he was induced to move away, he did so with reluctance. Under pressure he increased his pace to an

Fore-feet of Koala.

ungainly, lumbering trot, and the boy laughed aloud. Reaching the back of a tree, he started to climb as quickly as he could. The boy tried to beat him off, but luckily the stick broke. Just out of reach Booraby stopped, and, clinging to the straight bole, looked down with solemn, indignant eyes at his persecutor until that person departed. Then he climbed down again, and shuffled off to another tree which had been hollowed out by bush fires.

At the entrance, Kojurrie, the Goanna, raised his black head in surprise. Booraby, treating him with contempt, continued straight on, and the Goanna, thrusting out his forked tongue in resentment, doubled round to make way for him. Under a root, he saw Bogi, the Blue-tongued Lizard who regarded that hollow as his private residence. Paying no heed to him, the Koala selected a spot against the back wall, and curled himself into a big ball of fur and went to sleep. Bogi stuck close to his sheltering root, and kept a suspicious eye on the unwelcome visitor as long as he remained on the premises.

At sundown, Booraby was abroad again. With deliberate steps, he made his way down to a little creek where a half-submerged log afforded him an easy drinking place. He lapped the water up somewhat after the manner of a dog. Except for drinking purposes, he did not like water. He preferred a dry clean any time to a bath. Then he wandered leisurely about, but never wandered very far in any direction. He finally ascended a white box tree, where he remained until the following evening.

With the approach of winter, a change came over him. He saw other Koalas going about in couples, and it struck him all at once that it was a very good idea. Chancing to meet a young lady Koala on the ground, he squatted down in front of her, and gave the matter long and serious consideration. Her large, soft eyes were expressive of a kindly, gentle nature. She was a lady of striking appearance, well able to take care of herself, and, at the same time, able to afford him such companionship as he needed during the winter evenings. Undoubtedly a partnership would be beneficial. But he was not a creature who rushed to conclusions. He studied her, and meditated.

For a long while, they sat there without saying a word. Then the maiden got up to see about supper, and, with the same grave, contemplative air, he strode after her. A gruff voice down the hole in front of them woke him up. Was she going to see that fellow? With feelings of jealousy he ranged alongside, and, uttering a few soft grunts, edged her off in another direction. In a retired spot, he started up a small tree, and looked back at every step to see if she were following. But she passed on in search of a better tree; so he backed down again, and hastened to catch up to her.

A dallying hour brought them to a big blue gum tree. Among the branches, there was a comfortable hollow knob. He led the way up to a stout limb that was overhung with clustering leaves. He was a good judge of positions and of the weight-carrying capacity of branches. Once only had he been at fault. It was a brittle branch, and he had crept out a little too far. He fell so heavily that he bounced, and, for some minutes afterwards, he sat there blinking sulkily at the cause of his fall.

They had spent so much time on the ground, that day dawned upon them as they finished their repast. Toonool, the lady Koala, curled herself up in the hollow, whilst Booraby wedged himself in a smooth fork near her. When night came again, he descended with her to the ground. Thenceforth they lived together, and the blue gum was their home.

Toonool slept nearly always in the hollow, and rarely appeared in the open before night. As for her partner, he seldom sought a hiding place, and was often wandering about on the ground in broad daylight. Occasionally, he did not come home in the morning, and she was anxious about him, especially when she heard the howls of the dingo pack, or the furious barking of hunters' dogs. Either daylight surprised him at a distance, when he decided that it was too late to go home, or he was too tired and sleepy to climb to the considerable height at which their domicile was situated.

One evening, when the cold weather was departing, Mrs. Koala emerged with a baby on her back. Booraby surveyed the newcomer with grotesque solemnity, and, in his quiet, unassuming way, was pleased with the little maid.

When the cub began to walk about a little, he allowed her to climb over him, and, at times, he squatted down and lazily played with her. As she grew older, he turned away from her with a bored expression, or checked her innocent playfulness with a growl. He drifted back into his solitary habits, and frequently occupied a different tree in the vicinity of his mate.

In the summer, his fur grew thin and shabby, but, with the returning cold season, it was replaced with a new coat. From this time to the end of spring he was at his best, and looked sleek and vigorous. In his new suit, and with his humorously-solemn cast of countenance, almost human in its expression, he was an attractive creature. He was thirty-two inches in length, eleven inches high, when he stood on all fours, and eighteen inches in girth. He now accompanied his partner more constantly than he had been wont to do of late. They were alone again, for Miss Koala had just gone off with one of their young neighbors, and the pair had made their home on a low ridge across the little creek.

Booraby, after drinking, sometimes wandered to that ridge. Rambling about there one sunset hour, he met the Wombat. This creature was a stout marsupial who was much like himself in form, but considerably larger. He was forty-four inches in length and seventy pounds in weight. Again, the Wombat had a short tail, while the Koala had none at all.

Warro, the Wombat, was so agreeable as to extend an unmistakable invitation to the gravely observant Koala to join him in his early evening repast of grass and roots. Although nocturnal in his habits, he not infrequently emerged in daylight. The dipping sun still shot rainbow shafts across the hill as he started to feed. The Koala grubbed up some roots beside him. Striking a good patch, he squatted down on his haunches to eat them, but the Wombat stood up at his meal.

At that moment, Mrs. Wombat emerged from the burrow and strode curiously towards the Koala. The Koala at once retired, and his expression and manner clearly conveyed what he thought: "One Wombat is tolerable, but two's a crowd."

She followed him a little way towards a gum sapling, and then stood and watched him ascend, as though she were impressed with his remarkable lack of smartness. She was not very active herself, and could neither leap nor climb. But, when a woodsplitter, looking for timber on his way to camp came along the foot of the ridge, she showed that she was not slow of foot. Her activity in scampering back to her burrow was a revelation of unsuspected speed.

The splitter's dog, when he arrived, nosed about with raised bristles. Discovering Booraby, he leaped at the sapling, and barked and whined in his excitement. The Koala was well out of reach, but, when the splitter, a moment later, drove his axe into the sapling, he looked up anxiously for a means of escape into another tree. Alas! no friendly branch was within reach.

A few vigorous strokes brought it down. He did not jump as the Possum would, but clung to his perch until the fall threw him sprawling on the ground. Before he had time to pick himself up, the dog's fangs crunched into the back of his neck. There might be some excuse for the offence of the dog, for he was only following his instincts, but there was none for the wanton action of the other brute, who had no need to cut down the useless sapling.

In a little while the slayers departed. They left a still, grey form by the felled tree, where a feast awaited Kojurrie, the Goanna, and Wahgan, the Crow.

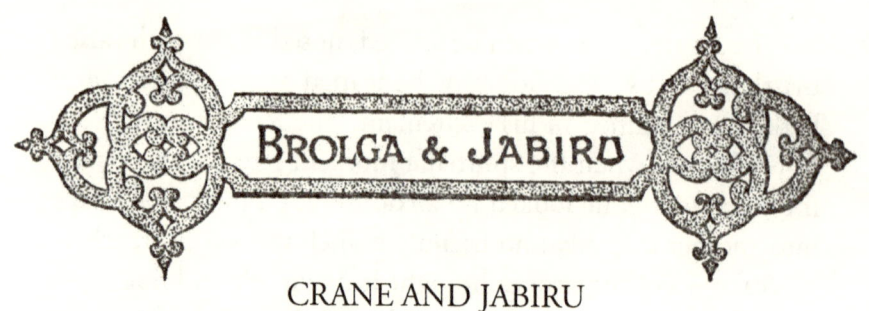

CRANE AND JABIRU

On a knoll in a shallow part of a big swamp was a heap of grass, reeds, and rubbish, measuring more than two feet in diameter, with a cavity six inches deep. It was the nest of the Great Australian Crane (the only true Crane in Australia), who was popularly known as Brolga or Native Companion. A few tea-trees were scattered about, and green reeds and odd clumps of rushes dotted the surrounding water. On one side were broad pools with great beds of tangled rushes, where the Black Swan, the Pelican, many kinds of ducks, and other water-fowl had their homes; on the other side a narrow plain, flanked by gum forests, extended for a couple of miles westward.

In the nest sat Wandi the young Brolga, and Moorooella his sister fledgling, and alongside squatted Kooroora the male parent, guarding the home while the mother bird was away feeding and collecting insects or vegetable substances for the infants.

A fine bird was Kooroora. He was four feet in length, more than four feet in height, and twenty pounds in weight. The Kio, or Plain Turkey, who equalled him in weight, looked small in comparison; and so did his friend, the Jabiru, or Black-necked Stork (Australia's only representative of that family), who shared the same marshy plain with him, for though the Jabiru was seven feet two inches across the wings when spread out, he very rarely exceeded fifteen pounds in weight. With all his length of pinion, he was otherwise less active than the Brolga, though on fine warm days he could soar quite as high as the latter, ascending high into the sky, and remaining there, far out of sight, for hours at a time. The Jabiru was a solemn bird, whereas the Brolga was a joyful creature whose loud voice was frequently heard in the localities he favoured.

Kooroora's deep-hanging throat pouch showed he was of great age. Exactly how old he was none could tell; it seemed to be a question between him and the Black Swan and the White Cockatoo, the longest-lived of the water-fowl and the perchers, as to which of them was the oldest inhabitant.

There had recently been heavy rains, so the waterfowl were numerous and jubilant. Another result was that farmer Slocum found his farm too wet to work, and came plodding round the swamp after ducks. On seeing him, Kooroora got up from beside the nest and walked away, making for the centre of the plain rather than for cover, and calling at intervals to his mate, who was not far away. The Jabiru was heading in the same direction; with his long red legs he strode quickly over the ground at a seemingly easy pace, keeping always at a safe distance from the gunner. His blackish-green and white plumage and huge bill made him a more striking figure in the landscape than the Brolga, whose silver-grey coat was more like the ground.

The farmer's dog, whilst rushing after waterhens, discovered the nest. Wandi watched him quietly as he splashed up to examine it. As soon as he came within reach, however, he shot out his sharp beak unerringly at the intruder's eye, which caused that animal, with frantic howls, to retreat hastily.

Then Slocum came on the scene to see what had caused the injury. Wandi was not disturbed by his presence. He was naturally sociable; he did not object even to the society of man, providing he was properly treated. Many of his kind lived in a half-tame state about the neighbouring farms.

What followed rather shook his confidence, besides leaving him with a feeling of loss and loneliness.

Slocum picked up Moorooella and tucked her under his arm.

"The old woman was saying the other day that she would like a companion," he remarked with a grin as he walked off with her. "This one should suit her as well as any; and ye'll be just as comfortable about the house, birdie, as ye would be out here. No telling what harm might come to ye in this place," he added, by way of excusing his act.

On his way home he stopped under the nest of the Jabiru. It was built in a tea-tree on the edge of the plain. The wood and twigs with which it was constructed would have filled a cart, some of the bottom pieces being as thick as a man's leg. In size it was bigger than the nest of any other bird, measuring fully four feet across and three feet in height. The top was almost flat, the very shallow cavity being lined with grass.

Being an inquisitive person, Mr. Slocum set the "companion" on the ground, and climbed to the top edge of the nest. At that point he was savagely attacked by two young birds, who were not visible from the ground. Smiling broadly he slipped down, with the observation that "he had only wanted to see what they were like."

They were big chicks, covered with long grey down, changing to the dark glossy colour of the full-grown one in the wings and tail. Their bills were then about six inches in length; the adult bill was ten inches long and two inches deep at the base. They were not quite ready to leave the nest; nevertheless, as soon as Slocum had gone, the old birds dropped them to the ground, and abandoning the nest, took them about with them on the plain.

A few days later Mrs. Brolga stepped proudly out of the swamp with her ungainly youngster striding awkwardly by her side. Though not actually associating with the Jabirus, they were never widely separated, while the undeveloped wings of the young ones confined their movements to that particular locality.

The Jabirus never wandered far from water, or off the wet plains. The Brolgas, on the other hand, showed as much liking for

(A. H. Mattingley.)

Wandi, the Brolga.

A Brolga's Nest and Eggs.

(*A. H. Mattingley.*)

the dry lands as for the marshy places. They really waded very rarely; in their habits of living partly on land and partly in the water they were more like the Spurwinged Plovers than the Blue Crane and the Egret. They favoured the open spaces, whence they made occasional short excursions into the thin forest in quest of lizards and insects.

Wandi soon learned how to catch them, but it took him much more time and practice to learn how to dig up the bulbous roots and other vegetable substances that formed a part of his diet. His powerful olive-green bill, which was six-and-a-quarter inches long, was well suited for such purposes.

At night they went to the vicinity of the nest, camping together on the ground. The knoll became drier and higher as the water receded. The spot was never very quiet, for the swans and ducks were active through the night, the Gnalgans, or Nankeen Herons, left their roosts for the marshes at dusk, moving about till dawn; and at intervals through the night the boom of the Bittern was heard in the grass and rushes. Then, too, the Muldries, or Magpie Geese, spread over the plains, waddling about in large flocks and chatting noisily. Their chatter at times kept the Brolgas awake; but the presence of these timid fowl was an assurance of absolute security from all harm.

Wandi exercised his big wings no more than a couple of times a day, sometimes only once, in a low, laboured flight from one end of the plain towards the other. Gradually he ascended higher, and when he saw over the tree-tops he became ambitious and vastly interested in the great green world that widened out beneath him, specked with numerous sheets and pools of water that glistened like diamonds in their emerald setting. Soaring on spread wings, he picked out the choice feeding-grounds and traced the courses of rivers and creeks that flowed through the glorious country. He saw many broad swamps that invited him, many a long lagoon and shimmering lakelet that charmed his eye.

His aerial excursions brought him into contact with other Brolgas. They came on to his plain until a company of twenty-five or thirty had gathered there, whom Kooroora captained with lordly pride. He had led his troops, generation after generation, through summer and autumn; sometimes he led them into mischief, as when his journeys, made necessary by scarcity of food, brought him near to a lucerne paddock, or close to wheat and barley fields. Coming out silently from the edge of the timber at sunrise, they picked up the newly-sown grain from the ploughed fields, and pulled up the young wheat and barley by the roots, afterwards departing in single file to a safe distance from the scene of their repast. If their camping place was a mile or more distant they flew to the paddocks, dropping down from high up in the air. Scarecrows, however cunningly made, did not disturb them in the least; and when the farmer's boy yelled at them and cracked his whip, they merely walked away with a leisurely step and a bored expression. The only thing that frightened them was a gun.

The gathering together again of the flock was celebrated at dawn with a dance. The old captain, with deep croaks, called his company together. With short flights the outposts drew in to one centre, the captain bowing gravely to each arrival. On these festive occasions, his most frivolous moments, he still endeavoured to behave with dignity, and amid the leaping and twisting of the giddy revellers the result was often very comical.

With his proud son at his heels he led the assembly, all marching round with stately steps and in perfect order, like dancers promenading in a ballroom. Suddenly they stopped, each standing still and straight. Then they bowed and scraped, partly crossed the circle towards each other, and bowed again. Some turned towards their companions in the line and curtsied, a big fellow occasionally bowing his head right down to his toes.

These first movements over, they set to partners, and performed a fantastic quadrille—hopping, prancing and jumping, always ending with the same grave and stately bow.

The performance varied from the grotesque to the artistic, from the graceful march to an ungainly goose-step, and from the superb making of perfect circles to a bewildering maze of intercrossing curves. To Wandi, who was capering and twisting all over the place, it was as beautiful as it was joyful.

Two birds would approach one another towards the centre. Sometimes they bowed and danced in a few artistic curves and circles round each other. At other times, after bowing (they were so polite they never forgot to bow), they backed away, then gave a jump and stood rigid on one leg, the other leg being stuck straight out behind. Setting it down suddenly, they began bowing again, which was followed by a sort of gallop, the birds jumping and leaping, twisting and turning, and going through a series of antics and drill movements until at last the captain gave a leap that showed his purple-black legs above the heads of his comrades. The proceedings then terminated abruptly, and the entire company marched away to feed, uttering an occasional croak.

Afterwards the dance became a regular morning festivity; occasionally the flock performed at other times in the day. They wandered from one feeding ground to another, camping at night in the edge of the timber. As they emerged at dawn for the dance and to arrange the day's programme, they shook out their long tails and wings, and smoothed their glossy plumage with their bills. Wandi gave as much attention to his toilet as the proudest belle in the company.

An aboriginal legend related that, in the long-past time of the Bunyip, the Brolgas learned to dance from watching the native corroborees. The black-man, proud of the birds' accomplishments and their wisdom, held them sacred.

The general colour of Wandi's plumage was silver-grey, darker on the back; the crown, bill, and the throat-pouch were olive green; the back of his head and a circle round the yellow eyes, coral red; the under parts of the smaller wings were dark brown, and the bigger wings black.

As the day warmed the captain rose with his company into the cooler air of the upper regions, rising gradually in wide circles until he became a mere speck; higher yet until he was entirely lost to the sight of creatures on the ground. At that vast height he floated slowly round and round on outspread wings, at intervals giving out a loud trumpet-call that went floating down softly to the earth. With a vast extent of country under his eyes, when he grew tired of floating in space, he soared directly down to the spot that took his fancy, though he was rarely absent long from his native plain.

On one of these excursions Wandi observed his sister at the farmhouse. She heard his cry, grating down through space, and became suddenly attentive. She had become quite a member of the household, roaming at leisure about the premises, through the garden, and over the farm-paddocks. Of a quiet nature, she was surprised at nothing she saw; neither was she afraid of anything she met with in her rambles. She had humbled the boss rooster in his own yard; she had sent the cat jumping wildly from her path, with his back up, spitting angry protests as he went; and she had caused the dog to leave his favourite spot and slink round the house with a dejected expression. In a sedate, dignified way, she went just where she liked, the undisputed mistress of the broad domain.

She had been quite contented; but that call from the clouds awoke the sleeping instinct of her race. Coming to her ears like a cry from her nestling days, it disturbed her strangely. Moving out towards the descending bird that called, she uttered a hoarse note in reply.

The farmer, seeing his wife was in danger of losing her companion, stepped out with a looking-glass, which he stood against the garden fence near enough to attract the bird's attention. As soon as she saw her reflection she stepped up close to it with a gleam of delight in her yellow eyes. Surely it was her long lost mother returned to her! She bowed to it, and was immensely happy when, thrusting her beak against the glass, the beak of the image seemed to touch her own. Standing close to the mirror, she began to vigorously clean and smooth her dress with her bill, paying no further heed to her wild relative, who had alighted on the flat.

With a smile of satisfaction at the success of his scheme, Mr. Slocum withdrew. But there was one disadvantage about that image; it would not follow her when she walked away. It seemed to turn tail and go in the opposite direction. She called, but still it went away. Anxiously she hastened back, and in moving about it she knocked the glass down on to its face. For once in her life she was astonished. She looked through the palings and peeped round the corner; but the new mate had completely vanished.

Just then Wandi called again. Moorooella had not seen him alight, but no sooner did she see him standing on the flat than she fancied he was the bird she had suddenly and mysteriously lost—of course he had flown down there! It was all quite clear; he wanted her to go that way. With a happy cry she went to him, and so once more she was a member of the flock.

They moved down the plain towards the swamp, where the mother Jabiru and her two big youngsters were fishing. The father Jabiru had gone off to another swamp, where he walked alone. He was more reserved than the Brolga, shyer and more retiring. He loved the swampy, open flats where little clumps of tea-trees abounded. There he caught fish, reptiles, tadpoles, and other small animal life that lived in marshes, resting between times in exposed places where he had a wide scope within range of his ever-watchful hazel eyes.

With the spring weather the solitary state became distasteful. He spruced himself up and returned to his old mate. His family of last season, though quite independent, were still "at home." They were pleased to see him; but he was not pleased to see them. He said: "Here, get out of this!" or words to that effect, and drove them away to find a home of their own.

Left to themselves, the old couple built another huge nest, twelve feet from the ground, in a tea-tree that stood well out in the swamp; and when two large, coarse eggs were laid, the old bird, Barry (the aborigines called him Barri-enna) shared with his mate in the duty of sitting. He did not find it a pleasing occupation, hatching eggs. Mulyan, the Wedge-tailed Eagle, took a mean advantage of him when he was thus occupied, attacking him so fiercely at times as to force him to leave the nest. He was a lover of peace and quiet, and such an outrage made him shake his long bill in moody resentment as he stood away off on the plain, watching until the greedy bird had departed from the neighbourhood.

Wandi, about the same time, found it advisable to quit his native run. The old couples had gone away to their different grounds. The youthful members gathered together and moved about in a discontented way until they began to find mates for themselves.

They had a dance at dawn on a clear level by the side of a winding lagoon. The performance differed somewhat from those of former occasions. It was more of a love-making gathering.

One of the males elected himself master of ceremonies, and endeavoured to lead the company in the march and through the quadrilles in the usual way; but his brother members were most of their time bowing politely to the stately grey hens.

Wandi, noticing a graceful lady just behind him as they marched along, turned round at once and bowed to her. He continued to bow until the others had passed on and they two stood alone. Then, rising to his full height, he moved stiffly and proudly up to her side, talking in soft gurgling notes, till their long necks, coming together, formed a cross. Next he sidled round her with short quick steps, bringing up in front of her again. For a while they stood together, looking towards their fellows at intervals as though reluctant to part, and between times fondly mixing their necks or running their bills along each other's glossy back. At last they moved off on a way of their own, now and again calling out "goodbye" to the company as they went.

There were so many new couples going into housekeeping that they visited many suitable localities before they found one that was not occupied, that is, by others of their own kind. Pairs of Blue Cranes, White Cranes, and White Ibis were in possession on the edges of the swamp; some Spurwinged Plovers and a pair of Jabirus were also there; and spread over the plain was a large flock of Black-and-White Ibis. But these did not matter, so long as they did not come too near the actual nesting spot.

This place Wandi chose for himself and his mate, and there he seemed to have put up a notice that "all trespassers would be persecuted," for "persecuted" they certainly were if they went close to his private abode.

There was no knoll sufficiently high for the purpose of a nest. Close investigation showed that they were below floodmark; so, choosing the highest knob that was to be found in a marshy situation, they raised it several inches by digging and heaping the earth with their bills. A hollow was formed in the centre, which was roughly lined with grass and roots, mixed with bark and small sticks. Two creamy eggs, blotched with chestnut and purple brown, and measuring three-and-a-half by two-and-a-quarter inches, were laid therein, and almost immediately the hen commenced to sit.

The conduct of the Brolga at this period was in strong contrast to his usual companionable nature. He attacked savagely any bird, animal, or snake that dared to approach the precious nest. But to his mate he showed every sign of the closest affection. When she went off to feed he kept zealous guard over the eggs, never leaving the place until she returned to them. Towards the end of the hatching he became still more attentive, taking his turn at sitting; and when the baby-birds broke out of the shells and held up their quaint little heads, he was even prouder than the mother. They were never left alone for a minute, for in the mother's absence he sat by the nest, watching them affectionately, and flashing angry glances towards all other creatures that appeared in the vicinity.

This regard for his offspring continued until they were nearly half grown. Then his interest in them gradually lessened, and for a time before the reassembling of the flock he was as often alone as in their company. Sometimes, after soaring to an immense height, he would make a sudden call on a neighbour; and the neighbour, announcing his coming with a trumpet call from the clouds, also dropped down for a visit on him. This meant that the notice against trespassers was removed. Very shortly they assembled in large parties, and wandered together, or in small companies, where they pleased, occasionally in dry times going far afield.

Except for occasional absences, when the community mingled together, Wandi remained year after year on the flat he had chosen for his home. Every year a new nest was made, but always near the same spot. Some seasons they nested as early as June, in other seasons the important duty was delayed till as late as November, the breeding-time depending much on the rain.

So he lived his simple life for many seasons.

www.ingramcontent.com/pod-product-compliance
Lightning Source LLC
Chambersburg PA
CBHW031155020426
42333CB00013B/678